Mastering
In-Line Hockey

THE OFFICIAL NIHA COACHING
AND STRATEGY BOOK

This book is available in quantity at special discounts for your group or organization. For further information, contact:

> Triumph Books
> 644 South Clark Street
> Chicago, Illinois 60605
> (312) 939-3330 FAX (312) 663-3557

ISBN 1-57243-108-3

Cover design by Mulligan + Mulligan.
Book design by Graffolio.

Credits
Cover and chapter opening photographs © Bob Messina.
Herb Brooks, player/coach format drawing, stretching exercises, referee signals courtesy the NIHA.
Equipment photographs: Skate, helmet courtesy CCM; Gloves, helmet, cage, jock shorts, bag courtesy Itech; Sticks, girdle, shin guards, shoulder pads courtesy Christian; Elbow pads courtesy Mission; Goalie equipment courtesy Franklin; Jerseys courtesy Hyper; Pants courtesy Hystk Sport.
Drawings for skills and equipment by Yvonne Tio-Tilleux.
Diagrams for drills and plays prepared by Hugo Garcia.

References
Canadian Hockey Association, National Coaching Certification Program (1986)
National In-Line Hockey Association, Risk Management Guide
National In-Line Hockey Association, NIHA Official Rulebook (1994)

Contents

Foreword

For many years, I have been involved in the great sport of hockey. Through my experiences, I have become absolutely certain about one important principle: competition without preparation is antidevelopment. This is where good coaching comes into play.

Over the past five years, the National In-Line Hockey Association has been diligently leading the charge in the development of a great new sport—in-line hockey. In 1992, while developing the official NIHA rule book, the founders of the NIHA looked closely at ice hockey to capitalize on all the positive aspects of the sport—speed, finesse, and excitement—while attempting to eliminate injuries, stoppages, and fights. The result is an alternate version of hockey that encourages participation for all age groups regardless of gender—the sport of in-line hockey as we know it today.

Since 1992, the NIHA has been actively promoting and fostering the responsible growth and development of the sport. Their latest contribution is in the pages that follow. Authors Brett Callighen and Ron Chipperfield, two former Edmonton Oilers, spent hours analyzing the game from the coach's perspective. The result is an excellent manual for coaches to develop individual player skills and winning team strategies.

Herb Brooks
Head Coach
1980 USA Olympic Ice Hockey Team

A Word from the Authors

As a ten-year veteran of professional hockey in North America with the WHA and NHL (Edmonton Oilers), and my European experience, I have developed a unique instructional/coaching philosophy. As a result, The Hockey Institute, Inc. was created—a new dimension in hockey training. My experience as a General Manager for the Toronto Planets of RHI (Roller Hockey International) has also encouraged me to contribute to this manual.

Like performers in any field of endeavor, coaches and players alike require the special training, tailored environment and mindset to help them optimize their potential to excel. I co-wrote this manual with Ron Chipperfield in order to provide the sport of hockey some of the positive training and mindset it has given me.

Brett Callighen
Owner and President of the Hockey Institute, Inc.
Consultant to the National In-Line Hockey Association

In writing this book, I pass on to you five years of junior hockey, followed by twenty-two years of playing, coaching, and managing professional teams in North America and Europe.

Some highlights in these years were captaining the Edmonton Oilers and being part of eight championship teams.

Hopefully my experiences, along with studying the in-line game, will enable me to pass on to you a better understanding of this new sport.

Ron Chipperfield
Coach and General Manager Bolzano Italy
Consultant to the National In-Line Hockey Association

ACKNOWLEDGMENTS

Chris Dal Cin, Associate Director
Olympic High Performance Centre, Toronto

Shawn Jones, Executive Director
National In-Line Hockey Association, Miami, Florida

Jackie Crux, Literary Consultant

Hugo Garcia, Computer Programmer
National In-Line Hockey Association

Joseph Mireault, President/Director
National In-Line Hockey Association

Yvonne Tio-Tilleux, Illustrator

Introduction

The National In-Line Hockey Association provides the amateur sport of in-line hockey with leadership and helps foster the development and growth of this popular recreational activity. The NIHA promotes the safe, fun, noncontact sport through a variety of programs and services, including a number of publications.

This guide, along with the *NIHA Official Rule Book*, will help coaches provide a positive, healthy environment where teamwork and friendly competition lead to fun and fitness for all who are involved in the sport of in-line hockey.

Our hope at the NIHA is that this guide will help new coaches be more comfortable in their role as leaders and will assist them in developing a program where both they and their players enjoy the excitement and exhilaration of playing the game to the best of everyone's ability.

1

Coaching

Why are you coaching? Is it because you developed an interest in the game while watching your child play? Or is it because you are a young athlete at the end of your playing career who wants to continue to be involved with the sport? Whatever led you into the job, hopefully you are in it because you like the challenges of working with young athletes.

Coaches' jobs vary as much as their reasons for becoming coaches. They range from volunteers to part-time assistants in park district programs to full-time paid professionals. All, however, share certain responsibilities, and the primary one is to do everything possible to ensure that the youths participating on their teams have a productive, safe, and enjoyable experience.

A key way to accomplish this is to approach the job with a positive attitude and to instill this in the players. A positive attitude contributes to a dynamic learning environment and becomes a cornerstone of personal achievement. Nowhere is this more true than in sports.

Many professional and Olympic athletes speak candidly about the positive changes in their performance resulting from contact with a youth coach who introduced them to concepts such as visualization and affirmation and helped instill a positive attitude within them.

As a coach, you can convey positive reinforcement to players in a number of ways. The key is to keep it simple, enthusiastic, and sincere.

Key phrases to reinforce good play and attitude:

- You've got it now!
- Keep working on it, you're getting better!
- Good thinking!

- I knew you could do it!
- Way to go!
- You must have been practicing! Great execution!
- You're really improving!
- I'm very proud of you!

■ WHAT IS A COACH?

Coaching is a multidimensional job with a variety of functions that requires a wide range of skills. Many coaches are very skilled in some functions but weak in others. Good coaches work to perfect their strong skills and improve their weak areas, just as players are asked to do.

Whatever their strong and weak points, coaches should be aware that they serve many roles when they work with players, assistant coaches, officials, or parents.

Teacher

First and foremost, a coach is a teacher. A coach's job is to teach the game and its skills in a proper and progressive manner. As coaches teach their players to interact as a team, they also teach them social, psychological, and physical skills that will transfer positively to other areas of their lives.

Good coaches remain current in advances in their sport, and in new communication and teaching methods. This helps them provide players with the skills and knowledge needed to set measurable, attainable objectives.

Communicator

Good coaches have good communication skills. The ability to communicate effectively and keep communication open between coaches and players, as well as between players, is critical for developing individual and team skills and performance.

Body language is an important communication tool, particularly in coaching. Gestures and facial expressions can impart either approval or disapproval, and coaches must be aware of what their body language is saying, particularly with younger, more sensitive players. When learning the mechanics of the game, a novice player takes great encouragement from a "thumbs up" by the coach after a new move is attempted, but can be devastated by a look of disappointment when the move is not perfect.

Organizer

Good coaches are well organized. Young players especially need organized practices where there is little time for misbehavior and inattention. A well-organized coach generally has few discipline problems.

Plan each practice session in detail, starting with instructions given to players and assistant coaches in the changing room before practice begins through warm-ups, drills, the main practice, and a debriefing when the practice is over.

In your plan, clearly define the role of each player during the practice. Note how each position interacts with other positions on the team. Also assign responsibilities to assistant coaches and team captains, and communicate those responsibilities to all the players.

Role Model

Players, officials, parents, and fans look up to coaches. All closely watch how a coach behaves and respond to it. The coach's behavior directly affects how players (and parents of youth players) relate to other players (both team members and opponents), other coaches, and officials. The coach's behavior toward others sets the standards for the behavior of the whole team.

A good coach is

- A good teacher who imparts knowledge of the game
- A good communicator who keeps communication channels open
- A good organizer who provides a structure for the players
- A good role model who sets the tone for the team and projects a positive attitude

---

■ ASSISTANT COACHES' ROLES AND RESPONSIBILITIES

Many coaches are successful because they recruit and work with skilled assistant coaches. Good assistants bring additional points of view to strategy sessions, help on and off the playing surface, and perform a number of clearly defined roles.

The success of the assistant coaches depends on how well head coaches define their roles and support them in their duties. The duties assistant coaches assume vary from team to team, but most conduct warm-up sessions, manage the physical conditioning program, and help run practice sessions. They also assume specific duties during games.

It is important that all players, as well as parents of younger players and members of the coaching staff, recognize the duties of each assistant coach and accept the authority and responsibilities that go with those duties.

Practice Sessions

Practice sessions run smoothly when the roles of all players and coaches are clearly defined. Head coaches should discuss the division of duties with assistant coaches before the season begins, so that everyone is productive and effective.

Assistant coaches routinely manage warm-up sessions while the head coach prepares performance objectives for the practice session to follow. Assistant coaches often supervise the conditioning programs for the team and for individual players, both on and off the playing surface. Assistant coaches can also provide one-on-one coaching in goaltending or puck handling during practice or assemble and train players to manage special situations, such as penalty killing and power plays. Occasionally, assistant coaches should design and run an entire practice session. This helps ensure that practices run smoother when the head coach is absent.

A good assistant coach helps in practice with

- Warm-ups
- One-on-one coaching
- Conditioning
- Special team situations

Games

Game time is tension time. The fast pace and crowd noise often make it difficult for coaches and players to communicate with each other.

Assistant coaches help the head coach focus on monitoring and directing the play. As the head coach is asking, "Are the planned plays working?" "Do the lines need to be changed?" "Is the other team using a strategy that requires us to adjust?" the assistant coach serves as a liaison between the players, officials, and the head coach. The assistant is more likely to focus on the individual performance of players, while the head coach is looking at the overall team play.

During games, the assistant coach may also provide alternatives when critical decisions are required on team strategy. Assistant coaches can direct line changes and monitor individual player performance while the head coach monitors and directs the team play. Assistant coaches can also record data and compile game and player statistics for later evaluation, monitor and report on the condition of injured players, and serve as a mediator when a parent becomes too vocal or interferes with the play.

A good assistant coach helps in games by

- Providing strategy options
- Directing line changes
- Monitoring individual player performances
- Recording statistics for later use
- Monitoring injured players
- Serving as mediator with vocal parents

2

Individual and Team Equipment

Individual players are generally responsible for purchasing all of their own equipment, but coaches must be knowledgeable about what equipment is needed, and where players or parents can purchase it.

Safety is foremost in the design of all standard pieces of in-line hockey equipment, and parents should be cautioned against sacrificing safety for budgetary reasons. If new equipment that meets all safety requirements is too expensive for a family, they should be able to locate good, used equipment at secondhand sporting goods outlets. Significant savings can be found at these stores, and the coaches and their assistants should be aware of what stores in the area are reputable and knowledgeable about in-line hockey gear. In fact, coaches should encourage parents of rapidly growing children to find used equipment, since children often will not get enough wear out of new equipment to make it worth the extra expense.

■ TYPES OF EQUIPMENT

Equipment falls into two basic categories, technical and protective. Technical equipment includes sticks, skates, and gloves, which players use to perform. Protective equipment includes helmets, pads, face shields, mouth guards, and other equipment that helps keep players from injury. All equipment, whether technical or protective, should fit well for comfort, safety, and performance.

Goalies and skaters use different equipment. Coaches should advise parents about the differences between the two and discuss which type of position the child will be playing before they purchase any equipment.

■ SKATERS' TECHNICAL EQUIPMENT

Skates

When choosing skates, players should consider whether the boot offers adequate protection (ankle support and toe protection) and whether the chassis is of a type appropriate for the level of expertise and play. The wheels should be designed for the type of playing surface (i.e., concrete, sports court) where they will be used.

Skates should be chosen that fit closely in length and at the ball and heel of the foot. Check to make sure the boot provides good lateral support and prevents the skater from wobbling.

Although most boots are molded plastic, stitched boots have grown more common with recent advances in skate design. Some manufacturers incorporate gel packs into the boot. The body temperature of the foot warms these packs, which then conform to the contour of the foot. Gel-pack skates should not be shared between players.

Figure 2.1
Skates

Some boots are designed for rockering, which is an adjustment made to boots and wheels that increases lateral mobility while turning. High- end speed is affected by this adjustment, which should not be attempted by novices. Players can ask their retailer about the pros and cons of the design.

Gloves

Gloves should provide good protection while allowing proper hand movement. To ensure a comfortable fit, the player should try on gloves while

holding a stick. Oversized gloves restrict puck-handling ability and should be discouraged.

Palms of gloves can be either soft or hard leather. Soft leather breaks in faster, but the glove will also wear out faster.

Gloves come with short or long cuffs. Short cuffs give greater flexibility to the wrist and enhance puck-handling

Figure 2.2
Gloves

skills, but more forearm protection should be worn with them.

Sticks

Sticks are made from a variety of materials—wood, aluminum, fiberglass, and composites. The type of material used in the manufacturing affects durability, cost, and performance. Players should experiment to find the type of sticks most suitable for their use.

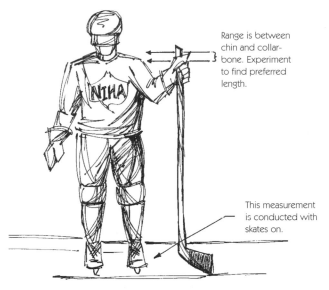

Range is between chin and collarbone. Experiment to find preferred length.

This measurement is conducted with skates on.

Sticks are made for right-hand and left-hand use and come in various lies. The lie is the angle formed where the blade and shaft of the stick meet, and it affects the way the blade meets the playing surface. The curvature of the blade also varies and sometimes can be customized to suit the individual player's needs

Figure 2.3
Stick length

The exact length of the stick is up to the individual. For beginners, a range is suggested between the chin and the collar bone when the stick is held upright against the body with the toe of the blade on the ground. A shorter stick allows for better puck handling, but it reduces the player's reach and may decrease the shot velocity.

Some players tape the knob of the stick to enhance grip and control.

As with skate wheels, the type of playing surface should be considered when choosing a stick.

Figure 2.4
Sticks

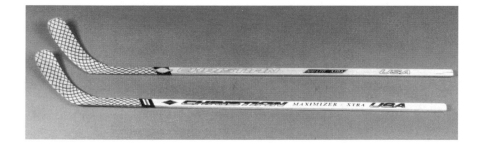

■ SKATERS' PROTECTIVE EQUIPMENT

Helmets

The helmet is the most important piece of safety equipment used by players and is mandatory for NIHA play. All players must wear a safety helmet to prevent serious head injuries.

Helmets are adjustable since a comfortable, snug fit is essential for safety. Only helmets approved by the HECC (Hockey Equipment Certification Committee) or the CSA (Canadian Safety Association) should be used. All players and members of the coaching staff should wear a helmet when on the playing surface.

Face Shields or Cages

All players up to eighteen in the NIHA must wear either a face shield or cage. Due to the risk of serious facial injury, the NIHA strongly recommends that all players, regardless of age, wear a face shield or cage during active practice or play.

Personal preferences usually determine whether players use shields or cages; the trade-off is comfort versus visibility. Shields are made of plastic and offer better visibility than a cage, but they tend to scratch easily and will fog up from time to time. They are also hotter. Cages are made of metal and are more resistant to impact than shields. They are also cooler, but visibility with a cage is more limited.

Most helmets are made to be worn with a specific shield or cage, and retailers can help players select compatible equipment. Shields and cages, like helmets, should be approved by the HECC, CSA, or the ATM (American Society for Testing Material).

Figure 2.5
Helmets can be fitted with either a face shield or a cage.

Elbow Pads

Proper coverage of the elbow and forearm is critical for protection against injury when players fall on hard, resistant, and often abrasive playing surfaces. When short-cuffed gloves are used, elbow pads must provide full coverage of the forearm.

They should be worn at all times, including during practice and warm-up. Elbow pads come in various sizes and styles, and, as with all equipment, the proper fit will provide the most safety and comfort.

Figure 2.6 (left)
**How to fit
elbow pads**

Figure 2.7
Elbow pads

Pants

Pants protect the thigh, tailbone, kidney, and ribs and are made in pant or girdle form. The pant form is a loose-fitting, Bermuda-style short with built-in padding. The girdle form also has built-in padding but fits more snugly and shifts less during play. A nylon shell is worn over the girdle.

Fit is extremely important in pants. A poorly fitting garment will not give sufficient protection, and pants that are too loose or too tight restrict movement and interfere with performance. Players should try on several styles and sizes before making a purchase.

Figure 2.8
**Girdles are worn
with a nylon
shell to cover**

Jock Straps and Jill Straps

This is a mandatory piece that players must always wear, whether in warm-up, practice, or in a game. Jocks come in two styles: jock strap and jock short. The jock strap has a separate cup and support. The jock short has

the cup and support built-in.

Both styles come in different sizes and proper fit is important. If the cup is too large, it will rub against the inside of the thigh, causing irritation. If it is too small, it will cause discomfort.

Jill straps, also called pelvic protectors, protect the female pelvic area and are sized according to waist measurement. Again, proper fit is crucial for proper protection. Another recommended garment for female players is the sports bra. Designed to reduce breast movement during active sports, it provides greater support than a traditional bra. They are available in standard sizes.

Figure 2.9
**Jock shorts
with built-in
protection**

Shin Guards

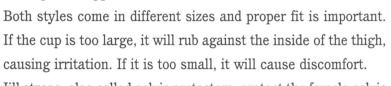

Figure 2.10
**How to fit
shin guards**

Shin guards protect the knee cap, shin, and upper portion of the ankle. They range in size from small to extra large, and fit is crucial for protection and movement.

The shin guard is held into position by using elastic Velcro straps or tape, wrapped around the shin pad below the knee cap and 3 to 4 inches from the bottom edge. Many players also tape around their socks to help keep the shin guard in place. Fit must be secure and slippage nonexistent. The bottom of the shin guard should just

Figure 2.11
Shin guards

overlap the skate tongue, either inside or outside, to ensure protection while allowing ankle and skate flexibility.

Shoulder Pads

The NIHA is a non-contact league; however, players should wear shoulder pads for protection against falls and accidental contact. Shoulder pads can be lightweight, but they should be strong enough to absorb impact. They come in a variety of sizes and styles, and cover shoulders, collar bone, upper chest, shoulder blades, and upper arms.

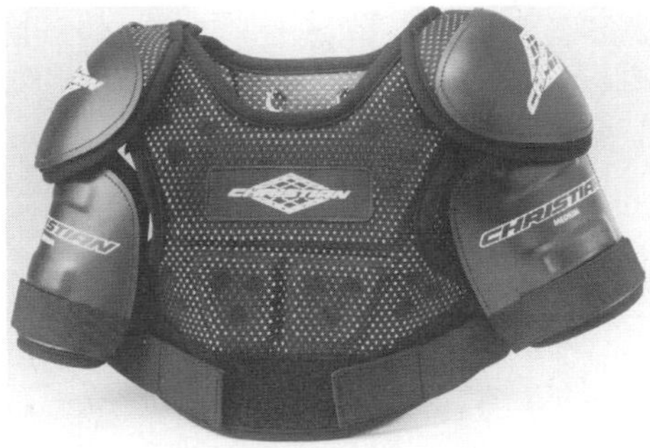

Figure 2.12
Shoulder pads

Mouth Guards

Recent studies have revealed that many sports-related brain injuries result from blows to the mouth and jaw. This type of blow is similar to an uppercut in boxing and can cause a concussion or swelling of the brain. Mouth guards help prevent these injuries and also reduce the risk of chipped and broken teeth.

The use of mouth guards is mandatory in NIHA play, and it is strongly recommended that mouth guards be worn at all times, including warm-up and practice.

There are several styles of mouth guards, including those available for players with corrective dental appliances (braces). The most effective mouth guards have rear shock-absorbers built into the device. Players can consult with retailers and coaches on the best type of mouth guard, and attention should be given to following the instructions for custom fitting.

Throat Protectors

Throat protectors protect the neck from stray sticks and pucks and are made from soft, pliable fabric that wraps around the neck like a collar. These are lightweight, adjustable in size, come in a variety of colors, and fasten at the back with a Velcro tab.

Although this is not a mandatory piece of equipment, the NIHA strongly recommends that all players wear a throat protector while on the playing surface.

Skaters' Protective Equipment

- Helmet
- Face shield or cage
- Elbow pads
- Pants
- Jock strap or jill strap (pelvic protector) and sports bra
- Shin guards
- Mouth guard
- Throat protector
- Shoulder pads

Skaters' Technical Equipment

- Stick
- Gloves
- Skates

■ GOALIES' TECHNICAL EQUIPMENT

Skates

Goalie skates provide greater protection than those worn by skaters. An extra-strength built-in toe piece and additional lateral protection shield the foot from pucks, sticks, and other players' skates. The wheels are smaller to allow for better balance and maneuverability. Proper fit in the length, ball, and heel is critical for maximum comfort, protection, and performance.

Sticks

Although goalie sticks are similar to those used by skaters, there are several significant differences. Goalie sticks are lighter in weight and more flexible than standard sticks, and the height of the blade is often customized to suit the individual goalie's needs. These differences help them make saves, deflections, and passes. Stick length depends on individual preference, but the stick should be long enough to enable the goalie to make an effective poke check.

Gloves

Goalies use two different types of gloves. The catching glove is designed to provide protection to the forearm and catching hand. It should be as light as possible while providing sufficient protection. Catching gloves come in a variety of styles and sizes and a goalie should try several types of catching gloves before making a purchase. The blocker glove is designed to protect the stick hand and forearm. Comfort and flexibility in the palm area are important for stick handling.

■ GOALIES' PROTECTIVE EQUIPMENT

Masks, Helmets and Cages

Helmets, cages, and masks are essential pieces of equipment for goaltenders. Helmets and cages worn with a mask must be approved by the HECC, ATM, or CSA to meet NIHA standards. Helmets and cages are adjustable.

Most masks are custom-made to conform to the contours of the goalie's faces. They have cushions built in to absorb shock and impact. These molded masks are more expensive. Goalies frequently paint their masks with distinctive logos and designs.

Goalie Pads

Goalie pads are designed for right and left legs, are lightweight, durable, and offer excellent protection to the lower leg. They come in a variety of sizes, styles, and colors. Note, however that there are regulations concerning maximum length and width, so players should consult with coaches and retailers before purchasing to make sure the equipment they are considering conforms to the rules.

Figure 2.13
Goalie equipment

Knee pads are often worn under the goalie pads. They cover the knees and protect the knees from injury on hard playing surfaces. They are available in a variety of sizes.

Arm Pads

Arm pads fit so that they protect the entire length of the arm and shoulder. Players should choose lightweight and flexible pads to allow easy movement.

Chest Protectors

Chest protectors cover the chest, ribs, and stomach areas. Players should choose protectors that are light enough to allow rapid, unobstructed movement.

Pants

Goalie pants protect the thigh, tailbone, kidney, and ribs. Like skaters' pants, they come either in pant or girdle form, but goalie pants are more heavily padded than skaters' pants since they experience more contact.

The pant form is a loose fitting, Bermuda-style short with built-in padding.

Again, fit is extremely important. A garment that is too loose or too tight can restrict movement or otherwise interfere with performance. Players should try on various styles and sizes before making a purchase.

Jock Straps and Jill Straps

Goalies wear the same type of jock or jill straps as skaters, but with extra padding for added protection. Again, fit is important for proper protection and comfort.

Throat Protectors

Throat protectors are the same for goalies and skaters. Although not mandatory, the NIHA strongly recommends that all players wear throat protectors.

Bags

All players will find they need a bag large enough to hold their equipment. Bags come in a variety of sizes and configurations.

Figure 2.14
Bag

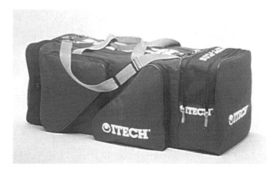

Goalies' Protective Equipment

- Mask, helmet and cage
- Arm pads
- Pants
- Jock strap or jill strap and sports bra
- Throat protector
- Goalie pads
- Chest protector
- Knee pads

Goalies' Technical Equipment

- Skates
- Catching glove
- Stick
- Blocker Glove

■ TEAM EQUIPMENT

First-Aid Equipment

The NIHA strongly recommends that all members of the coaching staff be certified in emergency first aid and that they consult with a first-aid professional when stocking their first-aid kit. Accidents do happen, and first-aid expertise will enable the coaching staff to deal effectively with emergency situations.

Team Uniforms

One member of the coaching staff should have responsibility for uniform maintenance and cleaning if possible. This eliminates problems caused by players forgetting or losing their uniforms and hclps control hygiene problems.

If the budget allows it, the team should have home and away jerseys. This helps to avoid the confusion caused when teams show up with the same colors for a game.

Practice Jerseys

Practice jerseys are also useful to have if possible. They help to extend the life of game uniforms. They can be color coded to help coaches and players identify practice teams during drills.

Figure 2.15
Jerseys

Water Bottles

The NIHA recommends that teams provide players with individual water bottles. This reduces the risk of spreading infectious diseases among staff and players. Two or three clean towels should be kept on hand during practices and games in case of injury.

Tool Kit

Equipment frequently needs repair, so it is important to have the proper tools to make repairs and adjustments during practices and games. The kit should contain:

- set of Allen keys
- tape
- spare nuts and bolts for helmets and pads with plates
- leather punch
- spare skate wheels
- adjustable screw driver
- pliers
- needle and thread
- goalie pad straps
- lubricant

Pucks and Balls

The team should have an adequate supply of pucks and/or balls to run a proper practice.

Team Equipment

- First-aid kit
- Practice jerseys
- Towels
- Pucks and/or balls
- Team uniforms
- Water bottles
- Tool kit

■ COACHES' EQUIPMENT

All coaches should dress in proper attire to promote a professional image for the team, and to help provide hands-on instruction to players. In addition, the standard equipment for coaches should include:

- skates
- gloves
- stick
- helmet
- whistle
- play organizer

■ EQUIPMENT AND MAINTENANCE CONTROL

For the protection and safety of players, both coaches and parents should conduct regular inspections of all equipment. Wear and tear or breakdown of equipment should be repaired immediately. If equipment is damaged beyond repair, it should or, in the case of required equipment, must be replaced before the player resumes participation to prevent injuries.

Skates, wheels, and bearings receive the most abuse of all equipment, and particular care should be given to their repair and maintenance. Skates, particularly those with stitched boots, should be thoroughly dried between wearings to keep the leather inner lining from rotting, which leads to premature breakdown of the boot. Wheels should be rotated and bearings cleaned regularly, as recommended by the manufacturer. Players should keep extra wheels in their bags at all times in case of breakdown during practices or games.

3

Player Skill Analysis

Coaches must be able to analyze the individual skills of their players and develop an instructional program to help each player improve weak areas while continuing to develop strong areas of play. Analyzing skills accurately and establishing skills development programs for all the players will help the coach earn the players' respect, and it also helps bind the team together as a unit. Then, as the coach assembles the team, the assessed skills of individual players can be considered, and the team can be built effectively around the players' strengths and weaknesses.

Not all coaches have the luxury of an assistant coach, but if so, it will be much easier to evaluate players. During the assessment, the assistant coach runs the activities on the playing surface while the head coach observes and evaluates players from the sidelines. This makes note-taking much easier and allows the head coach more opportunities to observe and evaluate during play.

If the team doesn't have an assistant coach, other observers outside the team can be sought during assessments. Impartial observers, which can include coaches from other teams, more advanced players or knowledgable parents whose children are not involved in the assessment, can help the coach make difficult decisions on which players to select for the team or how to organize the players who have signed up.

Both assistant coaches and impartial observers offer different perspectives that may either reinforce or question the coach's initial assessments. Making considered use of such feedback ensures that the coach looks at all possible options while selecting or organizing a team.

■ SKILLS TO ANALYZE

Not all players are strong in all skill areas, and one job of the coach is to balance the team by selecting players who complement each other in strengths and weaknesses. Both tangible (size, speed, skating, stick handling, etc.) and intangible (team play, mental toughness, etc.) aspects of a player's skills must be taken into account during the selection of a team.

■ INDIVIDUAL AND TEAM SKILLS

Coaches evaluate players on their skating techniques, their success at executing passing and shooting drills, and their defensive techniques. An assessment of all potential goaltenders should be made at this time.

The coach observes the player in a game or scrimmage format in order to make any sort of accurate assessment of a player's team skills. Things to look for include the player's ability to work with teammates, how well they adapt to the playing style of others, and whether they will pass up a chance for individual glory if it will benefit the team.

■ PHYSICAL SIZE AND MENTAL TOUGHNESS

Physical size and strength is important in hockey and should be evaluated in all players. Moving a bigger forward back to defense, or a small defensive player up to a forward position, should be considered if it will help the makeup of the team.

But physical skills and stature are not the only measure of players' abilities. Competitive sports also challenge the mental toughness and ability of players. Players need to be prepared for the psychological pressures they will face during stressful game situations, and they need to be able to understand complex game strategies designed by the coaches.

Players should never be forced to take a position that they don't want to play. A player will more often than not adopt a new position smoothly if his or her skills match the position's requirements. However, if a player consistently objects to playing a new position, allow the player to stay in the original position. To do otherwise is to risk the player losing interest in the game.

■ HOW TO RELEASE A PLAYER

Some coaches, particularly those of traveling or all-star teams, occasionally have the unpleasant task of releasing players. The situation should be handled with diplomacy and tact to preserve the coach/player relationship. The coach should speak privately to the player being released, giving the player a chance to voice his or her thoughts. The coach should strive for a positive ending to the meeting so the player feels his or her self-worth has been recognized.

Player Assessment

- Individual skills
- Mental toughness and abilities
- Team skills
- Physical size and speed

4

Organizing Practices

A good coach runs well-organized practices that give all players an opportunity to participate fully and to further their skill development. This not only better prepares the team for game situations, but also lessens the number of discipline problems during the season. To achieve well-run practices, coaches must always be on time and prepared. This gives the coach the basis for demanding the same of the players.

As a role model, the coach should always strive to present a professional image to the players; one way this can be accomplished is through careful attention to dress. Both parents and players are turned off by a coach who presents a sloppy image. Equipment that a coach needs to run a practice—helmet, skates, stick, whistle, and gloves—should be maintained in good condition as an example for the players. The coach also should have a way to organize the practice—a clipboard to keep detailed notes, plays, practice schedules, and instructional references. Coaches should never underestimate the impact that a good or bad "image" has on a coach/ player relationship.

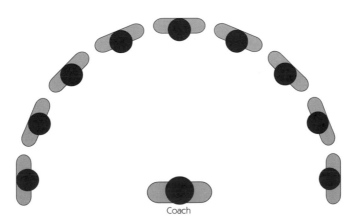

Coach

Figure 4.1
Suggested player/coach format for on-surface instruction

At the beginning of practices, the coach should state as concisely as possible, clear objectives for the session to players and assistants. A good way to do this is to gather the players in a half-circle with the coach in the middle and the assistants behind the players. This gives the coach eye contact with everyone and keeps players from becoming distracted.

Coaches and Practice

- Always be on time and prepared
- Present a professional image
- Communicate practice objectives

■ PRACTICE STRUCTURE

A well-designed practice progresses in a logical order from warm-up to cooling off. Each segment should be clearly defined so the players know what is coming next.

Warm-up

Warm-up exercises prepare players for the practice session and help prevent injury. Start the warm-up slowly and speed up the pace until all stretches are complete and muscles are warmed up and limber. Be sure to include the goalies in all warm-up exercises. Assistant coaches frequently handle this portion of practice while the head coach organizes the rest of the practice.

Instruction

Prepare the objectives and format of the practice beforehand, using a clipboard or similar device to hold notes. Presentation of the objectives must be short and concise. Players need to stay limber for the practice to avoid injuries, and they will cool off during long talks.

Drills

Always begin with individual drills and proceed to team-oriented ones. Assistant coaches can give individual instruction during drill time, while the coach maintains the pace and focus on the practice objectives during this segment of practice.

Play

Present specific coaching objectives in simulated game situations so players can practice them under pressure similar to what they face in games. Individual guidance should be provided by assistant coaches or the head coach when improvement in skills or performance is required.

Cooling Off

Cooling off exercises are just as important as warm-up exercises. Muscles that have not been allowed to cool down properly can stiffen painfully. Cooling off sessions can be conducted off the playing surface to conserve precious practice time on the playing surface for the development of core skills and techniques.

Good physical fitness will enhance a team's performance. Fitness follows from a well-organized practice with plenty of drills and game-situation play, but a conditioning program prescribed for players outside of team practice is also a good idea.

Practice Structure

- Warm-ups
- Instruction
- Drills
- Play
- Cooling off

■ FITNESS AND CONDITIONING

The coach is directly responsible for the physical conditioning of the team both on and off the playing surface. The coach must stress the importance of maintaining good physical condition year-round and help players develop an off-season program that will prepare them for the upcoming season.

Any sport is more fun when players are in good physical condition. Performance suffers and players are more suscpetible to injury when they are not in shape.

Fitness and Conditioning Program

Coaches should develop conditioning programs for players that can be followed both during the season and the off-season. These programs can be individualized to help players improve their performances on the playing surface and to minimize injuries.

Upper Body Strength Training

A strength training program for the upper body develops muscles used in puck handling.

Balance Training

Balance is extremely important in skating. Off the playing surface, players can improve their balance by using a slide board.

Flexibility Training

Stretching exercises to increase the flexibility should be included in warm-ups and cooling off.

Agility Training

These exercises also should be included in both warm-ups and cooling off. Increased player agility will help with quickness and response time to the action in game situations; both with the puck and other players.

Leg Power Training

A strength training program for increasing leg power will help players increase their ability to accelerate quickly.

1 30 seconds each leg

2 30 seconds

3 20 seconds each leg

4 20 seconds each leg

5 10 seconds each side

6 30 seconds

7 30 seconds

8 20 seconds

9 3 times for 5 seconds each

Fig. 4.2
**Exercises for
warming up and
cooling off**

Endurance Training

Endurance is essential for strong play from the beginning of a game to the end. This can be achieved with regularly scheduled distance running and skating. Increased endurance also helps players recover faster after an especially strenuous game or workout.

Water

As players engage in more strenuous physical activity during fitness and conditioning training and during team practice, the risk of dehydration increases. Serious consequences result from continued dehydration; players should be given water breaks every fifteen minutes during practices and a continuous supply of water should be available during the game.

• • •

Additional information on fitness and conditioning is available at your local library, retail bookstore, or health club. As a rule of thumb, it is always best to consult with a physician or a trainer when implementing a fitness and conditioning program. This will help coaches optimize their program and avoid injuries.

■ POINTS TO REMEMBER

Each coach develops his or her own techniques for running practices smoothly, but here are some important points and tips.

Fun

Encourage players to have fun. After all, it is just a game, and games should be fun. Research has shown that players work harder and accomplish more when the learning environment (that is, practice) is fun.

Be Flexible

Practice sessions may not always run true to form. More time may be required on a particular objective than was planned, but don't panic or rush the players beyond their abilities. Carry on, revising the practice slightly if needed.

Drill Book

Develop a drill book so that practices have sufficient variety and interest to hold the attention of players and coaching staff. Nothing is worse than always using the same drills every practice when there are numerous drills that develop the same skills.

Identify drills by names. Names save time as the players learn the drills by name they can move into position more quickly with fewer instructions. This also gives the coach an opportunity to assess the popularity of specific drills. Listen to which drills the players greet with enthusiasm and which ones they seem to dislike.

■ PLAYING WITHOUT THE PUCK

Players spend very little time actually handling the puck during a game. In order to best help their team, players must learn to play effectively without the puck.

Anticipation

An effective player skates to where the puck is going, rather than to where it is. This skill of reading the game situation may take years of watching and playing to perfect, but novice skaters can learn to interpret the play and react to the puck accordingly.

Drills intuitively teach players to anticipate where the puck will go. Players also can work on anticipation during the practice of set plays, since they will have the advantage of knowing where the puck is supposed to go.

Communication

Players should communicate with each other both on the playing surface and on the bench. On the playing surface, players ready to either pass or receive a pass should communicate with their teammates verbally, letting them know what is coming. They can also signal readiness to pass or receive a pass with their sticks.

On the bench, players should discuss their previous shift and current action on the playing surface with their line mates. This helps evaluate play and often leads to improved team performance.

Offense on Attack

Players should never coast on attack. Instead, they should always keep their legs moving when not in possession of the puck. This makes it more difficult for the opposition to read incoming passes and keep players in check.

Slot Play

The front and side areas of the net to the top of the face-off circles, called the slot, is where most goals are scored. Even when not in possession of the puck, players should head in the direction of the slot in anticipation of passes and rebounds.

Defense Position Play

Since a goal saved is just as important as a goal scored, playing without the puck is just as important on defense as it is on offense. The key to playing defense without the puck lies in a player's ability to play position hockey.

A sound defense requires conscious effort and discipline on the part of players; they must avoid taking risky offensive gambles when the odds are against them. Such gambles often leave them out of defensive position. The best defensive players have an ability to maintain their defensive positions rather than always playing the puck.

Goaltending

Goaltenders also must learn the advantages of playing without the puck. Concentration is a key for them since they often stand alone in the defensive zone for long periods while the action is on the other end of the playing surface.

The goalie must learn to stay focused during these periods. Since the goalie is in a position to see things teammates can not see, he or she can contribute to the overall team performance through good communication with teammates. Such communication can prevent critical mistakes or save a goal. Goalies who work with their teams in this manner are a real asset.

■ USE OF VIDEO FOR EVALUATION

Although not every coach has video cameras available for taping practices and games, those who do find that taping is a great way to critique both team and individual techniques and strategy. This is particularly true when instructing how to play without the puck.

Coaches should always review tapes before they sit down with the team to critique its play. During the critique, discuss what worked during the game or practice and what didn't. Coaches then can schedule future practice sessions to work on the team weaknesses.

Coaches and players both benefit from this training tool because it provides everyone an opportunity to assess play objectively and in detail.

■ SLOW LEARNERS

Every team has slow learners who require adapted coaching techniques. If necessary, drill these players individually (with an assistant if possible). Instructions need to be clear and evenly paced. Break each skill or technique down to the smallest steps. Demonstrate skills to reinforce each learning point. Then put the individual steps of a sequence together.

These players require frequent reviews, and learning objectives should be summarized for them after making the presentation to the group.

Slower learners can sometimes be paired off for drills with a friend on the team who has more advanced skills. A friend can provide additional encouragement.

Be patient with these players. Invite them to ask you to explain what is not clear and follow through with a detailed explanation. Listen, spend extra time with them, and offer geniune praise and encouragement and they may surprise you with their performance as the season progresses.

5

Seasonal Planning

At the beginning of each season, the main objective of the coach must be to increase the level of play in individual players and the team as a whole. This is true whether you are working with novices or with a team of professionals.

To achieve this objective, the coach develops short-term and long-term goals. Long-term goals are the hardest to stay focused on, but the coach can help players recognize that working hard and playing well during the season will reap long-term rewards. The coach can set a variety of seasonal goals that may serve as building blocks for the entire season. These can include reaching a certain number of wins in the season, attaining more goals scored than allowed, making the playoffs, or winning the championship. Striving toward these goals can be a source of constant motivation for the team.

Players and coaches both find it somewhat easier to concentrate on short-term goals. When the season is broken down into smaller segments (daily, weekly, monthly, and quarterly), it is easier to maximize concentration and focus on acquiring a specific skill during a practice or winning a special game.

Although it is the coach's responsibility to develop goals and strategies that the team can realistically achieve, players should be encouraged to set individual goals as well. Goalsetting begins in the preseason and continues on through the playoffs.

■ SEASONAL STRATEGIES

Preseason

First and foremost, the coach should concentrate on conditioning during the preseason. This will prepare players both physically and mentally, preventing injury and building confidence. Conditioning workouts should stress strength, agility, endurance, power, and speed—all are important for in-line hockey. A poorly conditioned team is the direct result of poor coaching and is unlikely to reach many goals.

Another integral part of any conditioning program is nutrition. An athlete's performance can be dramatically affected by the foods consumed during the season. Most players, particularly young ones, lack the knowledge necessary to make informed nutritional decisions and fail to understand the impact nutrition has on their performance. With guidance from their coaches, players can avoid making the mistakes of eating a large meal just before a game or eating excessive amounts of junk food.

Coaches can encourage healthy eating habits and help players monitor their diet during the season. They can do this by:

- Assessing the current eating habits of the players.
- Providing the players with proper dietary information for improving their eating habits.
- Offering nutritious drinks during practices and games.
- Maintaining an adequate supply of water at practices and games.
- Consulting with arenas and sports facilities where the team plays to encourage them to provide more nutritious foods and drinks.
- Inviting a sports nutritionist to speak to players and parents.
- Encouraging players to make gradual adjustments to their eating habits to bring about better conditioning.

Skill Development

Development of individual skills begins with the very first practice and should continue throughout the season. Team skills should be developed as soon as individual players have adequate skills to work as a team.

In-Season

The team should be in good condition when the season begins. The coach must remain vigilant and encourage players to maintain a high level of physical conditioning as the season progresses.

Individual skill development is a season-long process and should be worked on at every practice. Team skills and strategies take up more and more of in-season practice time and are necessary for a successful season.

Postseason

The best teams peak at the end of the regular season and reach postseason play at the top of their game, both mentally and physically. This is a pivotal time of the year where many teams fail to meet their long-term objectives and others far exceed theirs.

Coaches must become strong motivators in the postseason as they search for ways to help their team maintain a high level of enthusiasm and excitement that will help the players perform to the best of their abilities against strong opponents.

Seasonal planning
- Set long-term goals
- Set short-term goals

Seasonal strategies
- **Preseason**

  Conditioning

  Skills development
- **In-season**

  Maintain conditioning

  Improve team and individual skills
- **Postseason**

  Peak at the right time

  Stay motivated against strong competition

6

Individual Skills for Skaters

Coaches must teach players a variety of individual skills that range from basic to advanced skating, puck handling, passing, shooting, checking, and goaltending. Players seldom have the same level of skills in all areas and coaches must be able to arrange drills and practices so each player can work on his or her weakest areas.

Within each skill is a hierarchy, and certain skills must be attained before others can be practiced. For example, skaters must know how to attain a proper balance and stance before learning how to start effectively, and learning to stop comes after learning to start. All players must know how to skate before they can work on puck handling, passing, or shooting skills.

■ SKATING

Balance and Stance

Balance and stance are essential aspects of skating, and many coaches spend far too little time on them. Balance is directly related to stance; players must know how to achieve the correct stance for good balance both while learning to skate and while advancing to higher skating levels.

The proper stance for good balance is as follows:

- Keep head and chest upright.
- Maintain a slight forward lean in the upper body.
- Lead with the head forward over the knees.
- Position the chest over the knees.
- Align the knees over the toes.

- Grip the stick with one hand.
- Maintain shoulders, arms, and hands in a relaxed position.
- Place skates shoulder width apart.

The ability to maintain a proper stance and good balance can prevent falls from checks, collisions, or sudden turns.

Figure 6.1
Basic stance for good puck control

Figure 6.2
Skate wheels have inside edges and outside edges

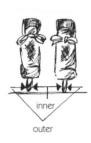

inner

outer

Arm Movement

Arm movement is another important part of skating. Improper movement negatively affects balance, leg extension, and physical output, which results in an overall poor performance. Lateral arm movement is counter-productive when skating; the stick arm should always move forward, using the same motion as in running, with the stick operating as an extension of the arm. A longer stick arm extension produces a longer stride. Forward movement of the free arm is directed ahead and upward, much like throwing a small uppercut. In the stick arm's backward motion, the elbow should brush the uniform while the free arm's movement should extend backward with a slight bend at the elbow. The wrist is turned in toward the hip with the palm of the hand facing up.

Figure 6.3
Arm motion

Movement of the free and stick arms should oppose one another; the skater can avoid lateral arm movement by keeping the blade of the stick in a straight forward and backward movement and at right angles to the playing surface. This must be accomplished with a full arm extension.

Starting and Acceleration

After skaters have learned how to attain proper balance and stance, they can learn how to start and accelerate quickly. The two most important starts are the forward hockey start and the V-start.

Forward Hockey Start

- Maintain proper skating stance.
- Push the power leg (back leg) through to full extension right to the toe.
- Turn the trailing shoulder and head in the desired direction as the leg is extended.
- Exaggerate the forward body lean.
- Bring the power leg over the lead leg and place on the playing surface.
- Maintain stance while the glide leg now quickly drives through and back (at this point the skater should be on the toes of the skates).
- Execute two or three backward pushes while on toes.

The skater should now be moving at full speed. It is important to maintain proper stride and arm movement during this maneuver. *Note:* Backward pushes are only performed on accelerated starts.

V-Start

- Maintain proper skating stance.
- Turn toes of skates outward.
- Place pressure on the inside edge of each skate.
- Thrust backward and to the side until one leg is fully extended.
- Execute a toe snap push once the leg is fully extended.
- Exaggerate the forward lean to maximize backward push (the harder the push, the greater the acceleration).
- Avoid standing up when coming out of the start.
- Complete the same sequence with the opposite leg using the same force until the desired speed is achieved.

The skater should now be moving at full speed. Again, it is important to maintain proper stride and arm movement during this maneuver.

Figure 6.4
**V-start
(quick start)**

Stopping

Although skaters generally spend time practicing strides before becoming too concerned about stops, it is a good idea to spend time early on working on correct techniques for stopping.

Snow Plow Stop

Figure 6.5
Snow plow stop

- Maintain proper skating stance.
- Position weight slightly forward.
- Simultaneously turn toes of both skates inward.
- Direct pressure toward the inside edge of both skates.
- Maintain inward pressure until a full stop is achieved. *Note:* At high speeds, alternate skate-to-skate pressure.

Hockey Stop

- Maintain proper skating stance.

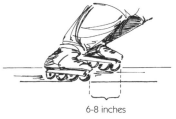

6-8 inches

Figure 6.6
Hockey stop

  - Commence a hockey stop by performing the initial functions of a power turn.
  - Maintain an open and staggered stance.
  - Rotate the outside shoulder in the direction of the stop.
  - Apply pressure to the appropriate edge of the skate to complete the stop.

As an example, for a left stop, the skater must apply pressure to the outside edge of the left skate and the right inside edge of the right skate.

The skater must push through on the left leg in the direction of the stop, and complete the stop as pressure is applied.

Toe Drag Stop

The toe drag can also be used as a speed control.

- Maintain proper skating stance.
- Drop the trailing leg behind the lead leg so that it is almost fully extended.
- Maintain the lead leg in a bent position and the chest in an upright, forward position. Hips and back must be facing in the direction of the stop.
- Turn the toe to the rear skate downward to apply pressure on the playing surface.
- Continue to apply pressure and drag the skate back and forth laterally until stopped.

Figure 6.7
Toe drag stop

Backward Snow Plow or Inverted V-Stop

- Maintain proper skating stance.
- Turn knees and toes out.
- Turn the heels inward.
- Apply pressure gradually to the inside of the knees and down to the inside of the skates until the stop is completed.

Figure 6.8
Backward snow plow

Inverted Backward T-Stop

- Maintain proper skating stance.
- Position the body similar to the forward toe drag stop while moving backward.
- Exaggerate the forward lean.
- Fully extend the back leg with the inside of the boot almost touching the playing surface.
- Apply pressure to the inside edge of the backward skate until the stop is completed.

Figure 6.9
Inverted backward t-stop

Stride Development

After a skater has learned to start, he or she must learn to maintain a proper stride while skating forward and backward.

Forward Stride

- Maintain proper skating stance.
- Start the leg push with skates close together (starting position).
- Fully extend the power leg, pushing the skate to the side, not backward.
- Complete the extension with a toe flick.

Figure 6.10
Forward stride

Figure 6.11
Acceleration

Skaters should try to keep the glide leg in the proper stance and strive for a quiet (not heavy) stride. When the skater completes a full stride, the skate should be lifted, but kept close to the surface. The skater should retract the foot to the glide position and repeat the sequence for the opposite side. Skaters who push back will find their stride shortened, and tend to lose control of their balance and work harder. Skaters tire much more quickly with a poor stride than with a correct one.

Backward Stride

- Maintain proper skating stance.
- With the power leg, push off the inside of the skate wheels.
- Push out and diagonally forward from the body, fully extending the power leg through to the toe.

- Draw the heel backward, creating a half-circle (a "c" cut) on the playing surface until the skates are shoulder width apart (back to the skating stance position).
- Maintain the glide leg in the skating stance position.

In this maneuver, the stick should be in the top hand only and the blade should remain on the playing surface.

Figure 6.12
Backward stride

Crossovers

While striding either forward or backward, skaters should learn how to make crossovers.

Forward Crossovers

In the forward crossover, the skater should turn with the stick extended ahead of the player.

- Initiate the turn with the outside shoulder.
- Fully extend the power leg.
- Pick up the power leg.
- Place the power leg over the glide (inside) leg.
- Maintain an inside leg bend (skating stance) until the glide skate touches the floor.
- Push laterally with the inside leg on the outside wheel edge through to full extension.
- Maintain a skating stance with the outside leg.

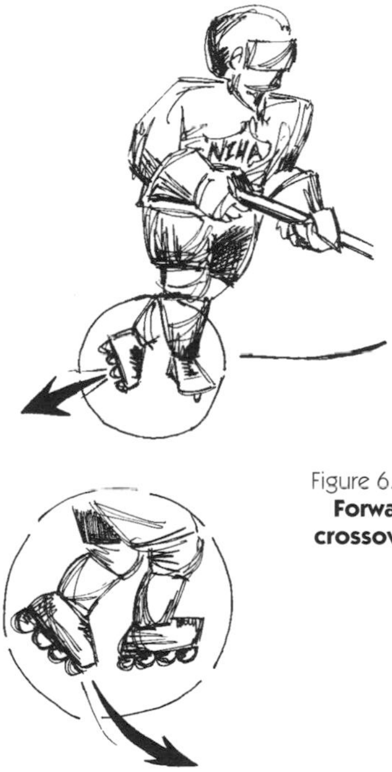

Figure 6.13
**Forward
crossover**

The proper execution of a forward crossover maximizes speed and minimizes energy output. Higher speeds create a lower center of gravity. Also, the speed of the turn directly relates to the degree of forward lean achieved in the crossover.

Backward Crossovers

- Maintain a proper skating stance.
- Move the hips and shoulders as a unit in the direction of the turn.
- Push out laterally with the power leg to full extension.
- Pick up the power leg and place it over the inner skate.

- Touch the floor with the power leg.
- Keep the inner leg bent (skating stance) to maintain balance and maximize the inner leg push.
- Push laterally with the inner leg through to full extension on outside wheel edge.
- Maintain outer leg skating stance position.
- Bring the inside leg back to retrace the original path to the skating stance.

The proper execution of a backward crossover maximizes speed and minimizes energy output. Again, higher speeds create a lower center of gravity, and the speed of the turn directly relates to the degree of lean achieved in the crossover. The stick should be held in the top hand and the blade should remain on the playing surface.

Power Turns

Skaters also can make use of power turns, where the stick enters the turn first, followed by the hands, outside shoulder, and inside leg.

- Maintain proper skating stance.
- Lead with the left leg to turn left; lead with the right leg to turn right.
- Evenly distribute weight between the front leg and the trailing leg in a staggered stance.
- Turn the head and shoulders in the direction of the turn.
- Make a quick shoulder and arm rotation to produce a faster turn.
- Commence crossovers halfway into the turn (which then becomes the acceleration or power out of the turn).

A properly executed power turn uses a high degree of lean and quick shoulder and arm rotation, since a low center of gravity will reach higher speeds.

Note: When turning to the forehand side, the stick is pushed away from the body and the top hand is pushed through and under the bottom stick hand. When turning to the backhand side, push both hands ahead and away from the body and into the direction of the turn. In both turns, the blade of the stick should by cupped in the direction of the turn.

Transition Turns (Mohawk)

The skater can be moving forward or backward to execute the Mohawk turn (also called a step out). A change of direction (left or right) is determined by lifting the corresponding leg in the desired direction. While making a right turn, for example:

- Maintain proper skating stance.
- Pick up the right skate.
- Turn the toe of the right skate outward.
- Rotate hip, outside shoulder and head to the right.
- Bend the glide leg in the skating position and keep skates at right angles to each other.
- Place right skate on playing surface.
- Exert pressure with glide leg on the inside edge of the opposite skate.
- Push off into the direction of the turn.

When executed properly, the hip, shoulder, and head should rotate 180°. The power leg should also rotate 180° and face the desired direction.

Individual Skating Skills

- Proper Stance
- Forward Hockey Start
- V-Start
- Snow Plow Stop
- Hockey Stop
- Toe Drag Stop
- Backward Snow Plow or Inverted V-Stop

- Inverted Backward T-Stop
- Forward Stride
- Backward Stride
- Forward Crossovers
- Backward Crossovers
- Power Turns
- Transition Turns (Mohawk)

■ OFFENSIVE PUCK-HANDLING SKILLS

Puck-handling skills are second only to skating skills for in-line hockey players. Some players compensate for merely adequate skating skills by developing outstanding puck-handling ability.

Puck Control

Players must learn to control the puck while moving forward and backward.

Figure 6.14
**Basic hand
position**

Forward Puck Control

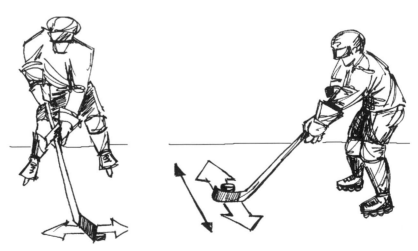

While moving forward, skaters should:

- Maintain proper skating stance.
- Hold the stick firmly in the upper hand using a V-grip position.
- Keep the lower hand loose to allow a gliding movement up and down the shaft of the stick.
- Hold the stick away from the body to allow a full range of motion while keeping the head up.
- Cup the puck with the stick and roll the wrist side to side for control.
- Avoid slapping the puck or banging the playing surface with the stick.
- Move up the playing surface (in no traffic) with the stick arm extended up and diagonally away from the body on the stick arm side.
- Maintain the position of the puck on the backside of blade.

Figure 6.15
**Basic stick
handling**

Players should develop puck-handling skills in both quick lateral motion (shoulder width apart) and broad full arm extensions.

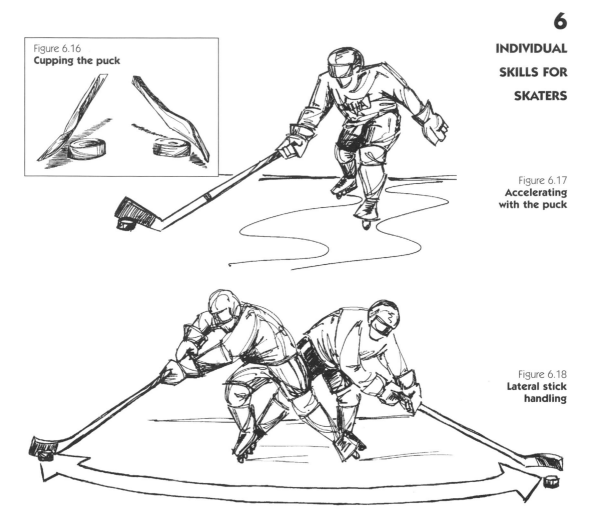

Figure 6.16
Cupping the puck

Figure 6.17
Accelerating with the puck

Figure 6.18
Lateral stick handling

Backward Puck Control

The procedures for backward puck handling are similar to forward puck handling.

- Maintain proper skating stance.
- Pull the puck diagonally and backward on each wrist roll.
- Move the puck from the heel on the backhand to the toe on the forehand to execute a backward wrist roll.

Diagonal Puck Control

Players use diagonal puck-handling skills with forward and backward crossovers. This allows them greater versatility when trying to elude opposing players.

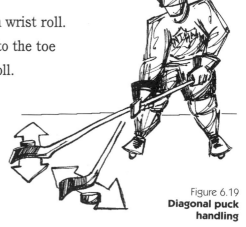

Figure 6.19
Diagonal puck handling

- Maintain proper skating stance.
- Move puck on a diagonal line as far forward to as far backward as possible.

- Increase the reach on the backhand by extending the stick forward in one hand while accelerating around the opposing player or protecting the puck.

Turning with the Puck

When making a turn, the puck should enter the turn first unless the player is protecting the puck from an opponent.

- Maintain proper skating stance.
- Roll the wrist, trapping the puck on either the forehand or backhand side of the blade.
- Look for a clear path before executing the turn.
- Use the technique for a power turn to complete the movement.

The blade must be kept closed during the movement, since the puck will roll off an open blade.

Protecting the Puck

It is important that players learn how to protect the puck from opponents.

Figure 6.20
**Protecting
the puck**

- Maintain proper skating stance.
- Pull the puck to the side of the body farthest away from the opponent.
- Fully extend the arms.
- Cradle the puck.
- Keep the body between the opponent and the puck.
- Shield the puck with the knee closest to the stick of the opposing player.

Skaters should maintain a clear line of vision throughout this maneuver. When the player is confident with stick-handling skills, one hand can be used to control the stick while the free arm shields the puck from the opponent.

Offensive puck control

- Carrying the puck forward
- Carrying the puck backward
- Controlling puck while skating crossovers
- Turning with the puck
- Protecting the puck

■ DEKING

Deking is using the body to fake out an opponent so a skater can break free for a shot or pass. Each deke requires its own special movement to be effective.

Head Fakes

Since opposing players constantly attempt to anticipate the direction of the play, this move is used to trick the opposing player into moving out of position, thus giving the offensive player an opening. The head moves laterally in one direction, signaling a turn, while approaching the opposing player, and the body drives in the opposite direction to go around the defensive player.

Body Fakes

Body fakes can be combined with head fakes to great effect. The body moves in one direction to draw the defensive player out of position, and the offensive player then quickly moves in the opposite direction. This is an excellent way to elude a check from an opposing player.

Stick Fakes

An offensive player can wave the stick laterally over the puck without moving the head or the body to cause an opposing player to misinterpret the intended play. After the defensive player bites on the fake, the offensive player can then make the intended move.

■ PASSING

Passing is a key element in team performance. The team's ability to pass and receive the puck ultimately controls the game and its movement. It is essential that all players are introduced to the different types of passes and receive instruction on when and how to use them.

The key to a successful pass is directing it to where the receiving player's stick will be, not to where it was. The player with the best passing skills is often the best player on the team.

Forehand Passing

- Maintain proper skating stance.

- Position hands in front of the body.
- Bring the puck across the body so that it is cradled on the forehand side of the stick.
- Sweep the stick through the swing, carrying the puck and rolling the wrists as the sweep continues until the puck is released.
- Transfer the weight from the power push leg through to the lead leg upon completion of the pass.

In both forehand and backhand passes, the follow-through of the stick in passing is just as important as the follow-through in shooting. The speed of the sweep and the roll of the wrists determines the velocity of the pass and the timing of the release of the puck.

Backhand Passing

- Maintain proper skating stance.
- Position hands in front of the body.
- Bring the puck across the body so that it is cradled on the backhand side of the stick.

- Sweep the stick through the swing, carrying the puck and rolling the wrists as the sweep continues until the puck is released.
- Transfer the weight from the power push leg through to the lead leg upon completion of the pass.

This pass is used infrequently since it requires considerable practice. However, once mastered, this pass is very effective because the motion involved masks the intent of the

Figure 6.21
**Backhand
passing**

pass. Most players, when on their backhand side, draw the puck to their forehand to pass it and thus telegraph the pass. Skaters who can execute a backhand pass open up more options.

Saucer or Cut Passing

The technique for the saucer or cut pass is the same as in the forehand or backhand pass, except that the puck leaves the playing surface, travels over an obstacle (e.g., a stick), and lands flat on the playing surface before arriving at its target.

- Maintain proper skating stance.
- Initiate the pass when the puck is at the heel of the blade.
- Move the puck up the blade to the toe of the blade.
- Release the puck.
- Curl the wrists to create the saucer effect.

Touch Passing or Redirection

- Maintain proper skating stance.
- Absorb or cushion the incoming pass.
- Execute an abbreviated forehand or backhand pass in the direction of the target.

Circumstances often dictate that a player must quickly redirect the puck to a teammate who is in a better position. An example of this pass is the give-and-go. In the give-and-go, the receiving player accepts the pass, passes immediately to an open player, and breaks to an opening to receive a return pass.

Receiving a Pass

- Maintain proper skating stance.
- Position the stick on the playing surface to provide a target for the passer.
- Ensure that the blade of stick faces in the direction from which the pass originates.
- Allow the puck to be cushioned or absorbed by the blade on impact.
- Always check the positions of the surrounding players before receiving the pass to develop an awareness of options.

Figure 6.22
Receiving a pass on forehand or backhand

Passing Skills

- Forward Passing
- Backhand Passing
- Saucer/Cut Passing

- Touch Passing/Redirection
- Receiving a Pass

■ SHOOTING

Players like to shoot, but as a coach you should emphasize that skating, puck handling, and passing skills are necessary to get players in the position to shoot. Only after they have mastered these skills should they begin to think about scoring. There are a number of ways to execute a shot, and each has its own specific purpose and use.

Wrist or Sweep Shot

This is the shot most used by in-line hockey players.

- Maintain proper skating stance.
- Keep the head up, face the puck, and keep the hands a comfortable distance apart on the stick so that adequate pressure can be applied to the shaft and the blade of the stick.
- Extend the arms forward, away from the hip.
- Position the puck at the side of body, behind the back skate.
- Cradle the blade of the stick over the puck.
- Apply downward pressure to the shaft and blade of the stick.

Figure 6.23
**Wrist sweep
shot**

- Initiate the shooting sequence by pushing off on the inside leg.
- Transfer weight from the back leg to the front leg.
- Complete the forward motion of the stick and puck with the arms, wrist, and hands in the direction of the target.
- Snap the wrists through the forward motion when the puck is even with the lead leg.

The wrist or sweep shot is complete when the hips, toe of the lead leg, and the blade of the stick are pointed at the target.

Snap Shot

The technique for this shot is similar to the wrist shot.

- Maintain proper skating stance.
- Keep the head up.
- Draw the blade of the stick back behind the puck to approximately knee height.

Figure 6.24
Snap shot

- Increase downward force by tightening the grip on the stick and hitting approximately 1 inch behind puck.
- Snap the wrists upon impact with puck.
- Follow through to the intended target.

The follow-through determines where the shot will go. The snap shot is complete when the hips, toe of the lead leg, and the blade of the stick are all pointed at the target. Timing is everything with this shot. The higher the stick is drawn, the longer it takes to execute the shot.

Flip Shot

The flip shot is widely used when play around the net is tight and the goalie is down. The player uses this shot to lift the puck off the playing surface quickly to clear an obstacle.

- Maintain proper skating stance.
- Position the puck at the player forehand or backhand side, slightly ahead of the inside leg.
- Place the hand low on the shaft of the stick in order to produce a higher shot.
- Scoop the puck with the blade at the point of contact.
- Raise the puck with the blade of the stick to the target area.

The quicker the scoop and follow-through, the quicker the puck is released. Shooters achieve the best results with good wrist and forearm follow-through.

Figure 6.25
Flip shot

Backhand Shot

The backhand shot is the most difficult shot and is used infrequently. However, it is the goalie's least favorite shot because it is very difficult to judge its direction. The backhand requires consistent practice due to its difficulty and because opportunities to use it in play are rare.

- Maintain proper skating stance.
- Keep the head up.

- Face the puck.
- Keep the hands a comfortable distance apart on the stick.
- Ensure that adequate pressure can be applied to the shaft and blade of the stick.
- Maintain a forward lean with the lead leg bent.
- Trap the puck under heel of the stick.
- Position the puck behind the back leg to initiate the shot.
- Apply strong downward pressure on the stick while executing a sweeping motion.
- Power push from the inside edge of the trailing leg and then transfer power to the lead leg.
- Roll the wrists and snap the puck when the stick blade is even with the lead leg.
- Complete the follow-through to the target.

The backhand shot is complete when the hips, toe of the lead leg, and the blade of the stick are all pointed at the target.

Figure 6.26
Backhand shot

Slap Shot

The slap shot is the most overused shot in hockey. It takes the longest time to execute, therefore making it easier to defend than most other shots. The slap shot should be the last shot in an instruction plan.

- Maintain proper skating stance.
- Center the puck between the legs and closer to the body than with other shots.
- Limit the height of the back swing to shoulder level.
- Slide the bottom hand down the shaft of the stick on the back swing.
- Slide the bottom hand up the shaft on the down swing.
- Maintain a firm grip of the stick on impact.
- Transfer weight from rear driving leg (power push) to the stick and then to the front leg when the swing commences.
- Contact the playing surface approximately 1 inch behind puck.
- Complete follow-through to the intended target.

The slap shot is complete when the hips, toe of the lead leg, and the blade of the stick are all pointed at the target.

Figure 6.27
Slap shot

One Timer

The one timer is similar to a slap or snap shot. The only difference is that the shot is made on a moving puck during a pass reception or rebound. The player may need to shoot from either the strong or weak side, and this dictates the body position or stance adopted by the player. When taking the shot, skaters should:

- Maintain proper skating stance.
- Keep the head up.
- Position the hands and arms tighter to the body with this shot than others.
- Wait until the puck is between the legs or advancing toward the back leg.
- Quickly hit the puck and complete the follow-through.

The moving puck and quick reaction time add a degree of difficulty to this shot, so it will take players lots of practice time and game sitations to master this shot.

Shooting skills
- Wrist or sweep shot
- Snap shot
- Flip shot
- Backhand shot
- Slap shot
- One timer

■ DEFLECTIONS AND REBOUNDS

Deflections and rebounds occur in the heavy traffic area in front of the net. Skaters develop timing and positioning for playing rebounds through trial and error.

Deflections

Players should always maintain proper skating stance when in the slot in front of the goal to ensure that they have an opportunity to play or control the puck after a deflection.

Incoming shots usually originate from the outer areas (i.e. the blue line, high in the slot, or outside hash marks in offensive zone). One forward should be positioned in front of the opposing team's net, outside the crease. This creates a screen and enables a player to redirect an incoming shot or pass.

Redirection or deflection also occurs when a player anticipates a shot to the goal by a passer. The player should skate to the net in order to redirect the shot. Players must maintain eye contact with the shooter and monitor activity around the net to make a redirection or deflection effective.

Rebounds

Many goals are scored on rebounds. When players take positions in front of the net and outside crease, they increase their chances of playing a rebound off the goalie or another player. Players can also drive the net for deflections to play a rebound. The ability to play a rebound improves the all-around quality of any player.

■ DEFENSIVE SKILLS

While the glory often goes to offensive players, games are more often won by great defensive plays. Strong checking and goaltending skills are the focal points of good defense, and coaches should work on these at least as much as they do on the above offensive skills.

Checking

NIHA league rules prohibit body checking. However, stick checking remains a very important defensive tool. Experienced defensive players learn to watch both the chest and the eyes of the opposition for clues about impending moves when stick checking. Eye and upper body movements often telegraph the offensive player's strategy.

Poke Check

Figure 6.28
Poke check

- Maintain proper skating stance.
- Hold the stick with the top hand.
- Keep the elbow of the stick arm slightly bent and close to the body.
- Wait until the opposing player enters the range of play (partial extension of the arm and the stick).
- Release the arm by extending the arm in the direction of the puck until contact with the puck is made with the blade of the stick.

Sweep Check

Figure 6.29
Sweep check

- Maintain proper skating stance.
- Wait until the opposing player in possession of the puck is within range.
- Wave the stick back and forth to create a sweeping motion. When executing a sweep check, restrict the sweeping motion to the wrists and arms. When players engage their shoulders in the sweep, they are more likely to upset their balance and miss the puck.

Lift Check

Figure 6.30
Lift check

This stick check is appropriate near a player who has possession of the puck or is about to receive the puck. The purpose of the lift check is to steal the puck or interfere with an incoming pass. While maintaining the proper skating stance, the player lifts the opponent's stick upward using the blade of his or her own stick in a lift check.

Stick Press

- Maintain proper skating stance.
- Direct the passer's shot to the opposing player.
- Apply firm downward pressure on the lower stick shaft of an intended receiver with the shaft of your stick.

The stick press check prevents the intended receiver from redirecting or deflecting the puck. This type of check is used most often by defensive players when guarding or defending the front of their goal.

Figure 6.31
Stick press

Back Checking the Open Man

For this important move, skaters should:

- Maintain a proper skating stance.
- Observe the game situation continually to be aware of changing situations.
- Stay between the puck carrier, the net, and the opposing player.

The desired position for back checking is about a stick length from the opposing player. See Novice Drill #4.

Angling

This check is most commonly used when approaching an opponent skating backward in a defensive roll. In this situation, the puck carrier should be forced at an angle toward the boards if possible. This limits the offensive player's options and forces movement that the defensive player desires.

The checker must not get too far ahead of the puck carrier, to prevent the offensive player from cuffing in behind the defender.

- Maintain proper skating stance.
- Take a position between the net and the puck carrier.
- Angle the opponent to the boards.

For a suggested practice drill, see Novice Drill #3.

> **Types of checks**
> - Poke check
> - Sweep check
> - Lift check
> - Stick press
> - Back checking the open man
> - Angling

7

Individual Skills for Goaltenders

Although goaltenders must use many of the same skills as other play-ers, they also use some skills only in the goal. Goaltenders should work on these skills during practices throughout the season.

■ BALANCE AND STANCE

The starting position for a goalie is known as the "crouch."

- Align shoulders and knees vertically.
- Distribute weight on the balls of the feet, while maintaining a slight bend to the knees.

Figure 7.1
Stance

- Keep chest up and slightly forward at the waist with the back fairly straight.
- Keep head up, extending out over the knees.
- Press the leg pads together, straight up and down (slight modifications are personal choice).
- Keep the catching glove open, out, and facing play.
- Hold the stick at right angles to the body so that the blade is square on playing surface. This will ensure that the blocker is up and ready for shots.
- Position the stick blade a few inches in front of the skates.

■ MOVING

Contrary to popular belief, a goaltender must be a skilled skater and should take part in all team skating and conditioning programs.

To move forward:
- Maintain the goalie "crouch" position.
- Push off the inside edge of either skate.
- Glide in the desired direction.

To move backward:
- Maintain the goalie "crouch."
- Keep the body square to the puck carrier.
- Push off the inside edge of either skate and glide in the desired direction

Goalies should use the snow plow technique to stop (point toes inward and apply pressure on the inside edge of one or both skates).

To move laterally (side-to-side):
- Maintain the goalie "crouch" position.
- Lead with the stick.
- Pivot the lead skate in the desired direction.
- Push off the inside edge of the trailing skate.
- Slow or stop by dragging and applying pressure to the inside edge of the trailing skate.

Figure 7.2
T-push

Figure 7.3
Shuffle

■ SAVES

The goalie must work hard to protect the net from the offensive team. When the puck is shot at the goal, the goalie must take defensive action to prevent it from entering the net for a score. The goalie can choose from a variety of actions to make a save:

Stick Save

- Maintain the goalie "crouch" position and a soft or loose grip on stick.
- Hold the stick with the index finger and thumb just above wide portion of the stick (where blade and shaft meet).
- Wrap the remaining three fingers around the shaft of the stick.
- Keep the stick to the front and away from the skates (this will provide a cushion on impact with the puck and help to reduce rebounds).
- Tilt the stick blade slightly forward.
- Move the stick in an arching motion from toe to toe.

Directing the Rebound

- Maintain the goalie "crouch" position.
- Maintain a firm grip on the shaft of the stick.
- Hold the blade of the stick rigid against the toes of the skates.
- Keep the blade of the stick upright with the heel of the blade resting on the playing surface.
- Direct the puck into the corners or to the side boards and away from opponents.

In directing the rebound, cushioning the puck is not required, as it is for a stick save.

Glove Save

The position and posture of goalies vary when making glove saves. The glove side is the goalie's strongest side, and a goalie with a quick glove can cover a large area. The wider the glove opening, the more space it takes up, thus decreasing the chance of the puck slipping by the goalie.

Figure 7.4
Glove save

- Keep the glove open, out to the side, and angled in front of body.
- Maintain visual contact with the puck until it enters the glove.
- Move the glove in an up-and-down motion.
- Move the body behind the shot (where possible) to act as backup in case the puck gets by the glove.

Blocker Save

Figure 7.5
Blocker save

As with a glove save, the position and posture of a goalie varies when making blocker saves.

- Move the blocker in the direction of the shot.
- Maintain visual contact with the puck until it makes contact with the blocker glove.
- Move catching glove to trap and freeze the puck against the blocker in one motion.

If there is no time to use the catching glove, the goalie should direct the puck away from the opposition or to a teammate in the immediate area.

Figure 7.6
Body save

Body Save

Move the body behind the shot (where possible) to act as backup.

- Use any part of the body to stop the puck.
- Maintain control of the puck to prevent rebounds.
- Position the body on top of the puck to smother rebounds.

Skate Save

Skate saves can be made with either skate, depending on the direction of the play.

- Begin in the goalie "crouch" position.
- Pivot the skate at a right angle to the direction of the incoming shot.
- Bring the knee of the trailing leg to the playing surface while the gliding skate is arching into position to stop the shot.

- Position blocker or glove (depending on the side of the save) slightly above the save skate in case the puck is shot high or skips above the skate.

Figure 7.7
Skate saves

Leg Pad Save

Although the position and posture of a goalie may vary when making this type of save, goalies should keep the leg pads facing the shooter as much as possible.

When moving laterally, speed is important since the movement turns the face of the glide leg pad to the side. This exposes the unprotected leg and increases the open space between the legs. The puck can then travel through the legs and into the net.

The goalie should attempt to direct rebounds off leg saves away from opponents.

Figure 7.8
Half-split save

Butterfly or V-Drop Save

This save is also referred to as a "five-hole" save.

- Initiate the save in the goalie "crouch" position.
- Move out in front of the crease.
- Keep the knees together.
- Drop to the inside of the knees.
- Lower and fan the legs outward.
- Keep pads flush on the playing surface.
- Center the blade of the stick between the pads to prevent a gap.

Figure 7.9
Butterfly save

Stacking Pads or Two-Pad Save

- Initiate the save in the goalie "crouch" position.
- Move to the right or left as required.
- Kick both legs out in the desired direction (as if sliding into home base).
- Stack the leg pads to create a barrier.
- Rest the top arm on the hip to increase the height of the barrier.
- Keep the bottom arm flush to the surface and fully extend the arm and stick laterally.

Figure 7.10
**Two-pad
save**

Playing the Angle

- Maintain the goalie "crouch" position.
- Move out from the goal in order to cut down the shooting angle.
- Remember the goalie relation to the net.
- Use different visual references on the playing surface to ensure proper positioning.
- Assess the positions of players on both teams.
- Prepare for either a shot or a pass.

Good forward, backward, and lateral mobility is essential for a goalie to be effective in playing angles. This will come only from repeated practice.

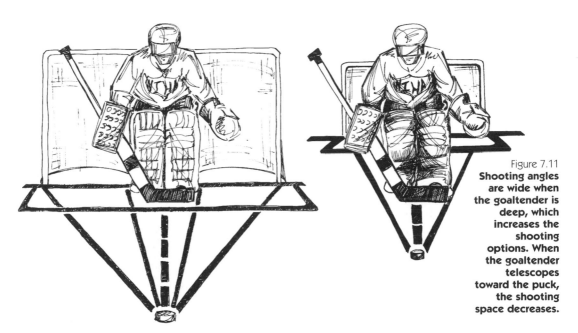

Figure 7.11
Shooting angles are wide when the goaltender is deep, which increases the shooting options. When the goaltender telescopes toward the puck, the shooting space decreases.

Poke Check Save

The position and posture of a goalie may vary when making these saves, which are effective when moving out from the goal to reduce the shooting angle. The goalie stick should have a good size knob to increase the effectiveness of this check.

- Hold the stick hand close to body.
- Maintain a bend in the elbow.
- Extend the arm and stick toward the puck quickly.

- Slide the shaft of the stick through the hand to grasp the knob at the end of the stick as the arm is extended.

Figure 7.12
Poke check save

Goalie Saves

- Stick Save
- Directing the Rebound
- Glove Save
- Blocker Save
- Body Save

- Skate Save
- Leg Pad Save
- Butterfly or V-Drop Save
- Playing the Angle
- Poke Check Save

■ GOALTENDING SITUATIONS

There are a number of situations where the goalie must make quick, practiced decisions to avoid allowing a goal.

Controlling Rebounds and Deflections

On rebounds the goalie must be prepared to cushion the puck with the stick or pads whenever possible and smother or freeze shots that cannot be redirected. After each save, the goalie should return to the crouch position.

Deflections

Goalies must always be on guard and prepared for deflections and redirection of the puck. The ability to balance forward and backward and to move laterally are important attributes that help goalies handle deflections.

To prepare themselves for deflections, goalies should always assess the position of opposing players in close vicinity of the net and be patient. They should also be careful not to move too soon and give an opening for the offense to shoot on the goal off a deflection.

Historically, puck handling, shooting, and passing skills have not been stressed in goaltending development and training. In today's hockey, however, they have become increasingly important, and a skilled goaltender who masters these skills can help the team in many ways. Coaches should encourage goaltenders to acquire these skills by including the goaltenders in team puck-handling and shooting drills.

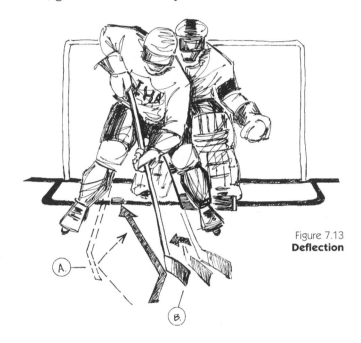

Figure 7.13
Deflection

Team and Individual Drills

Drills are divided into novice and intermediate categories. Keep in mind the team's skill level and run these drills accordingly, or split the team into novice and intermediate groups and run the two types of drills simultaneously if space permits.

For all of these drills, feel free to improvise. Players and coaches get bored with the same drills every practice. New elements will keep everyone on their toes.

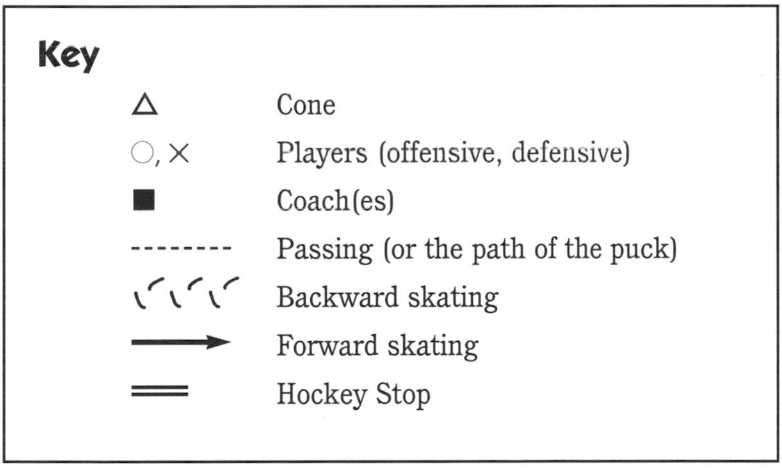

Figure 8.1
Key

Key		
△		Cone
○, ✕		Players (offensive, defensive)
■		Coach(es)
- - - - - - -		Passing (or the path of the puck)
⌒⌒⌒⌒		Backward skating
⟶		Forward skating
═══		Hockey Stop

■ TEAM WARM-UP

1. Players position themselves around the center circle and perform stretching exercises designed for the whole team. Have a different player lead the stretching at each practice.

2. Goalies participate in their prescribed stretching program and also take turns receiving warm-up shots from an assistant coach.

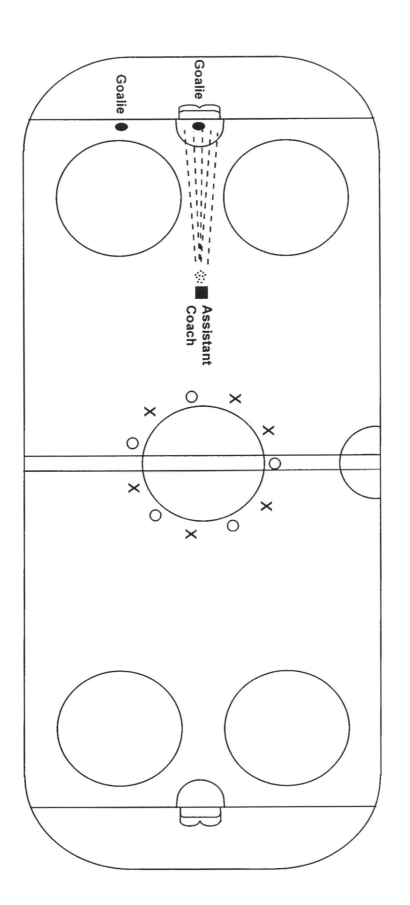

Goalie

Goalie

**Assistant
Coach**

Key

△
Cone

○✕
Players
(offensive,
defensive)

■
Coach(es)

Passing (or
the path of
the puck)

〱〱〱
Backward
skating

→
Forward
skating

═
Hockey Stop

Figure 8.2
Team Warm-Up

■ NOVICE DRILLS

Novice Drill #1

This drill develops the skater's passing, skating, shooting, and puck-handling skills. It is also a good warm-up for both the skaters and goalies. Keep the queues moving quickly so that skaters stay interested and to warm up the goalie and build confidence.

1. Split the players into two groups, one on each side of the red line. Each line should have a coach in the center circle.
2. The first skater passes to the coach and skates forward along the red line. When the skater reaches the coach, he turns toward the coach and skates backward diagonally toward the far circle.
3. When the skater reaches the blue line, the coach passes the puck. The skater catches the puck, turns, takes a shot, and moves to the end of the line. Shots should be taken no closer than the tops of the circles (or the hash marks for younger players).
4. After several repetitions, have the queues switch sides so that the skaters will have the opportunity to practice backhand passes and shots.

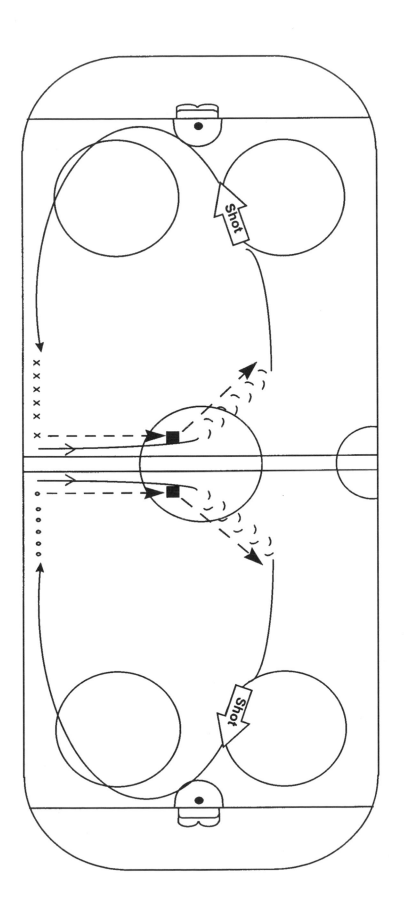

Key

△
Cone

○✕
Players
(offensive,
defensive)

■
Coach(es)

- - - - - - - -
Passing (or
the path of
the puck)

⌒⌒⌒
Backward
skating

⟶
Forward
skating

═══
Hockey Stop

Figure 8.3
Novice Drill #1

Novice Drill #2

The drills in this set are designed to develop individual skating and puck-handling skills. Execute these drills without pucks at first so that players learn the proper skating technique. Once they become familiar with the skating, introduce the puck. Alternate sides so that players learn to turn and stop in both directions.

Drill A

Set up a cone in the center of the circle. Players skate forward, execute a hockey stop in front of the cone, turn and accelerate, skating forward, back to the queue.

Drill B

Set up a cone across the floor. Players skate forward, execute a tight power turn around the cone, and skate forward back to the line.

Drill C

Set up a cone across the floor from the queue. Players skate up to the cone, step out forward to backward, and skate backward to the line.

Drill D

1. Set up one cone near the far side of the far circle and two cones, one at each side. Players skate forward to the center cone, turn, and skate backward around it to the right cone.
2. Players take a power turn forward around the right cone back to the far side of the circle, where they turn backward again and skate to the opposite cone.
3. Players then take a power turn forward around the third cone, skate around the center cone, and return to the queue.

Try setting up all four drills simultaneously and have the skaters rotate so that they can skate between drills and won't be standing for a long time. Keep the queues moving quickly to push the skaters to move faster and to keep them interested. Have the next skater begin when the one ahead is halfway through the drill so that they become accustomed to skating with others nearby. Improvise new twists to these drills to keep players interested.

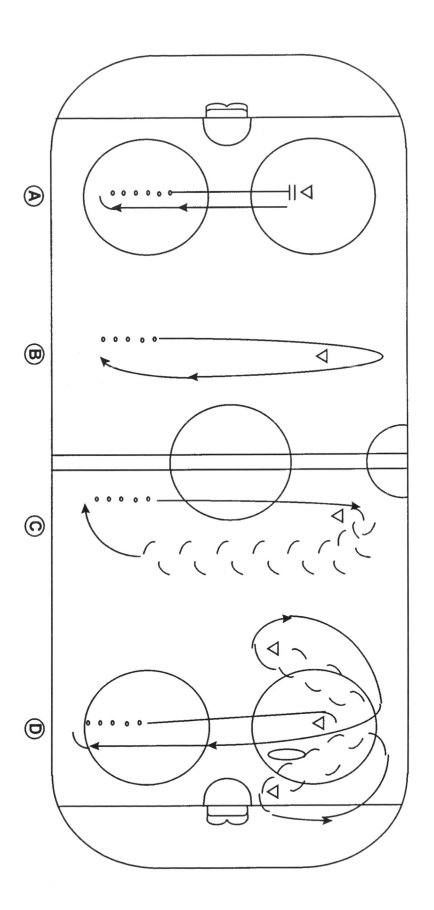

Key

△
Cone

○✕
Players
(offensive,
defensive)

■
Coach(es)

Passing (or
the path of
the puck)

〰〰〰
Backward
skating

➡
Forward
skating

══
Hockey Stop

Figure 8.4
Novice Drill #2

Novice Drill #3

These two drills can be worked simultaneously, one at each end. These drills are designed to work on defensive angling, protecting the puck, tight turns, and acceleration out of a turn. Stress proper skating technique throughout the drills. Drill A should come before Drill B, and players should alternate positions.

Drill A

1. Offensive players (forwards) queue up at the red line. Defensive players queue near the midpoint along the tops of the circles. A coach waits near the center circle.
2. The forward passes to the coach, who returns the pass—a give-and-go.
3. The defensive player skates up to the forward at the point of the pass (marked by a cone) and angles the forward away from the goal either by turning and skating forward or by stepping out and skating backward.

Emphasize that the defensive players should always be between the forward and the net. Begin this drill with the defensive players turning; as they gain confidence, have them try skating backward with the offensive player.

Drill B

1. The defensive players queue at the center circle. The forwards queue in one corner. A coach is positioned next to the goal.
2. The defensive player passes to the coach, who passes to the forward. The forward carries the puck around a cone near the red line and proceeds for a shot on goal.
3. Immediately after passing to the coach, the defensive player skates to a cone low near the coach, back around the high cone, and into position to angle the forward away from the goal.

This drill emphasizes speed and agility for both players and puck-handling skills for the forwards.

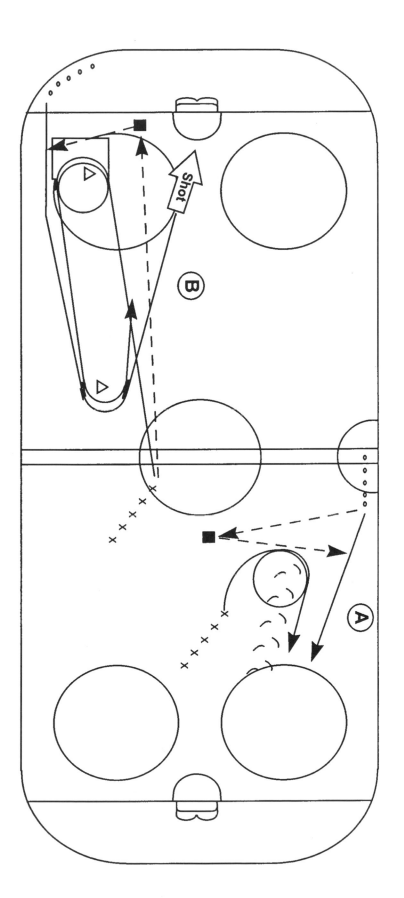

Key

△
Cone

○ ✕
Players
(offensive,
defensive)

■
Coach(es)

- - - - - - - -
Passing (or
the path of
the puck)

⌣⌣⌣⌣
Backward
skating

→
Forward
skating

═
Hockey Stop

Figure 8.5
Novice Drill #3

Novice Drill #4

This drill, called a two-on-one, utilizes all facets of the game. It is important that offensive players cover the entire playing surface, that passes are accurate, and that the highest possible speed is maintained. The final result should be a high percentage shot. This is also a good drill to allow players to read situations and make decisions quickly.

1. Defensive players queue up at the red line. Forwards form two queues at the blue line on each side. A coach waits in the far corner.
2. The two forwards skate toward the coach, constantly moving to get open. The coach passes to one forward, and both forwards break toward the far goal. Depending on the situation, the one forward can carry the puck all the way, or they can pass it to each other as needed.
3. The defensive player skates up to the blue line and skates backward into position to defend against the two forwards.

Emphasize that the defensive players must keep the gap between themselves and the forwards relatively small and should not back into or screen the goalie. The defensive player cannot commit to either forward, but should try to force a bad shot or pass from the player who has the puck.

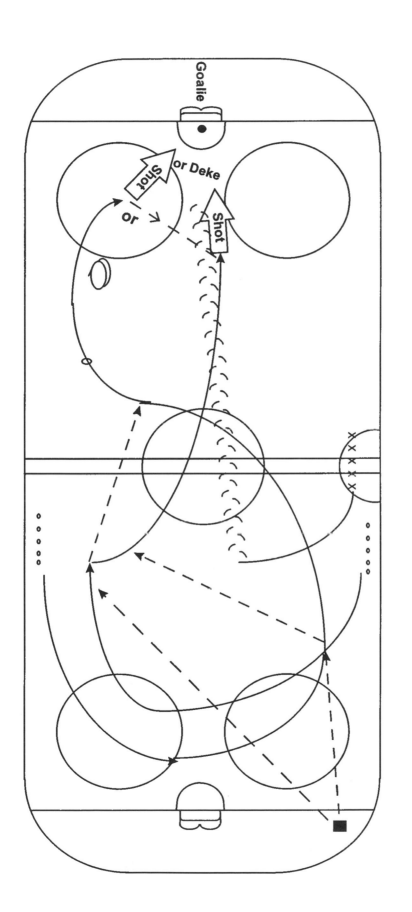

Goalie

Shot or Deke

or

Shot

Key

△
Cone

○✕
Players
(offensive,
defensive)

■
Coach(es)

Passing (or
the path of
the puck)

↶↷↶↷
Backward
skating

➜
Forward
skating

═
Hockey Stop

Figure 8.6
Novice Drill #4

■ INTERMEDIATE DRILLS

The intermediate drills take puck-handling, passing, and skating drills to the next level by emphasizing more advanced skills.

Intermediate Drill #1

This is a good drill for both players and goalies after the initial warm-up. It prepares all of the players for practice by emphasizing peripheral vision, heads-up play, making use of the entire playing surface, pass execution, skating, receiving passes, and executing quick shots.

1. Players queue up in four lines, two on each side of the floor between the red line and blue lines. Coaches should set up in opposite corners with pucks.
2. Play begins on both sides simultaneously when players from queues C and A pass across the floor to the opposite players D and B respectively.
3. Player B then passes up to C; player D passes to A while the first passers in queues A and C break out around the center circle to receive the pass from the next player in queue.
4. The breakout skaters take a shot on goal from the blue line, then receive a second pass from the coach close to the goal and quickly take a second shot.

Skaters return to the side of the rink they started on and queue up to receive and give a pass. After passing, players move over to the queue that skates and shoots.

It is important that players keep their heads up and know where to pass in each position. As long as players keep moving, this drill proceeds smoothly.

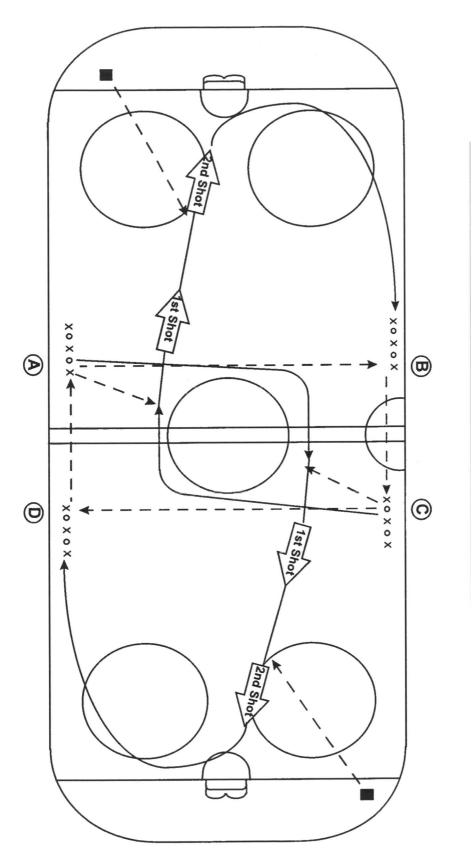

Key

△
Cone

○✕
Players
(offensive,
defensive)

■
Coach(es)

Passing (or
the path of
the puck)

ⁱ⸌⸌⸌
Backward
skating

→
Forward
skating

═══
Hockey Stop

Figure 8.7
**Intermediate
Drill #1**

Intermediate Drill #2

The drills in this set are good for advancing and monitoring individual skill development with and without the puck. Stressing balance and technique will help individuals to advance their skills.

Drill A

1. Players queue up in two lines facing each other at opposite circles. Set up two cones parallel to the goal with a stick balanced across them.
2. The first two players begin simultaneously and skate up to the cones. When they get close, they deke the opposite player several times, step over the stick, and skate to the other line.

This drill emphasizes deking and lateral agility.

Drill B

1. Set up a cone in or near the center circle. Players skate up to the cone, stop, step into a power turn around the cone, and return to the end of the queue.

Drill C

1. Set up a cone in the center of the circle opposite the queue. Players skate up to the cone, turn, and skate backward to the edge of the circle.
2. At the edge of the circle, they step into a forward power turn around the cone and skate back to the queue.

All three drills can be set up to run simultaneously. In drills B and C, emphasize acceleration out of the turn. When executing these drills with the players carrying pucks, emphasize puck protection.

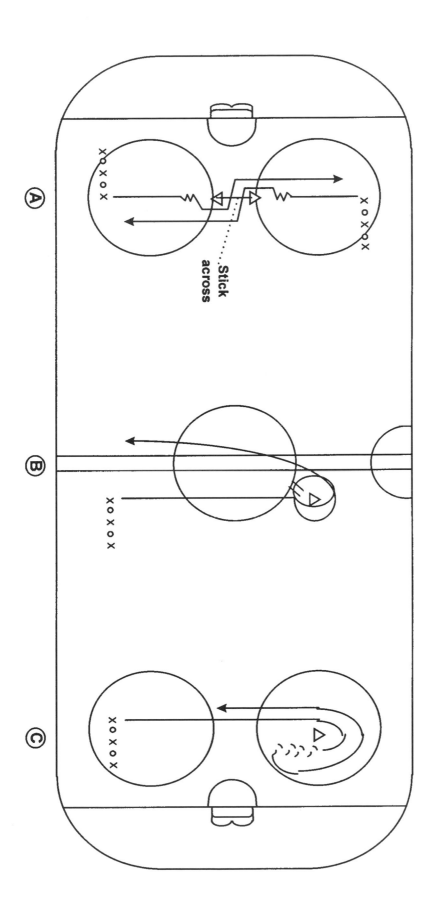

Stick
across

Figure 8.8
**Intermediate
Drill #2**

89

Key

△
Cone

○✕
Players
(offensive,
defensive)

■
Coach(es)

- - - - - - - -
Passing (or
the path of
the puck)

✓✓✓
Backward
skating

→
Forward
skating

═
Hockey Stop

Intermediate Drill #3

This drill works on passing, give-and-go, creating situations, and scoring. When the two-on-one is properly executed, the result is a high percentage scoring opportunity. Once the players are comfortable with the drill and its execution, it can be run out of both ends simultaneously. Heads up! Players should rotate in a clockwise format.

1. Forwards queue up in two groups on opposite sides of the floor (groups A and B). A queue of defensive players sets up near the center line (group C). A coach waits in the corner.

2. Players A and B begin at the same time, with player A passing the puck to the coach. The coach immediately passes the puck to player B, who shoots quickly and then proceeds to the net.

3. As player B is shooting, the coach passes a second puck to player A, who is cutting to the net. As soon as player A receives the puck, he or she directs a shot or a pass to the net so that player B can tip it in or take a shot.

4. Player C now proceeds toward the high slot, then steps out and skates backward away from players A and B. The coach passes a puck to player C, who in turn passes directly to either player A or B. They continue approaching player C on a two-on-one.

Speed, good passing, proper execution (use of the floor and timing), and quick release of the puck (shooting) should be stressed. Emphasize communication between the two forwards; encourage them to call for the pass and to get open for a good shot or passing opportunity.

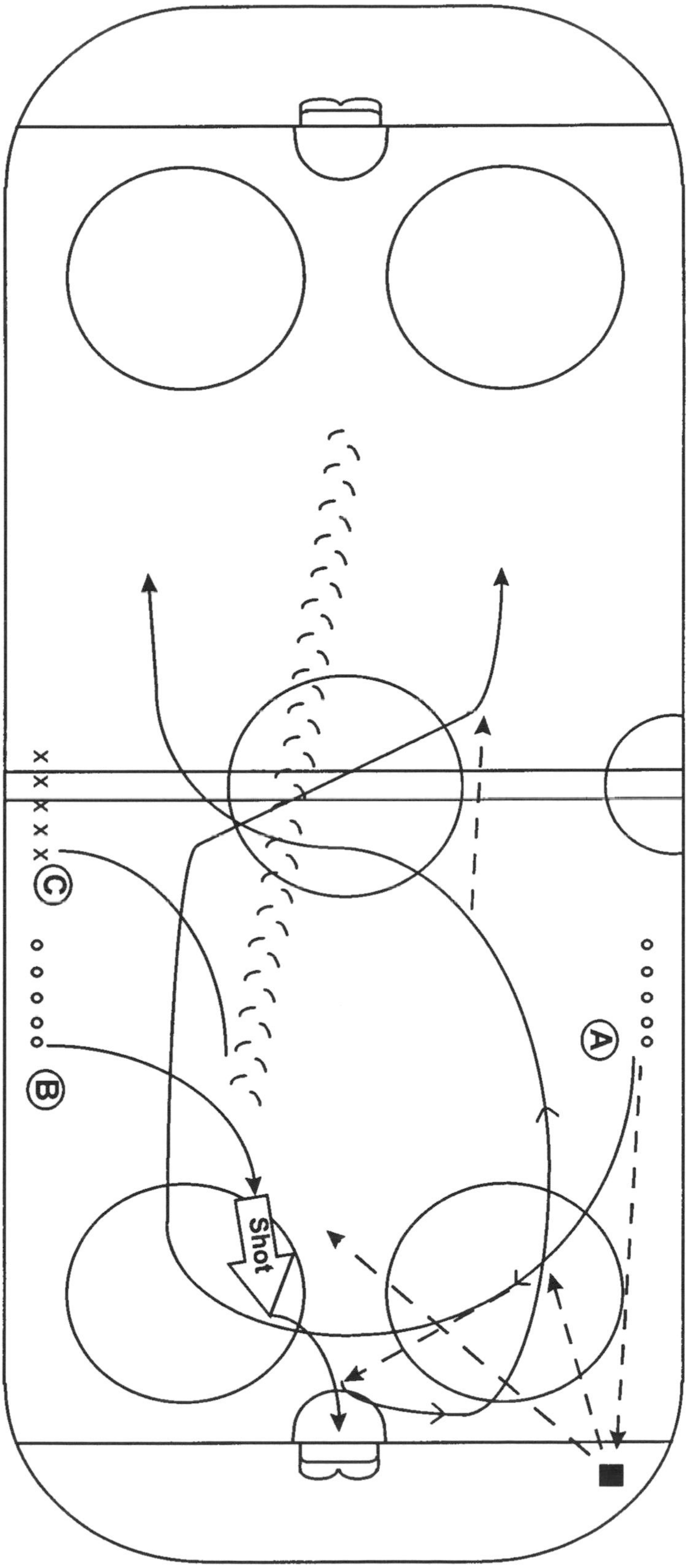

Key

△
Cone

○ ✕
Players
(offensive,
defensive)

■
Coach(es)

- - - - - - - -
Passing (or
the path of
the puck)

〳〵〳〵
Backward
skating

→
Forward
skating

═
Hockey Stop

Shot

Figure 8.9
**Intermediate
Drill #3**

Intermediate Drill #4

Both ends in this drill operate simultaneously. Stress constant movement, pass execution (both forehand and backhand), defensive players closing the gap, and heads-up play. Encourage the players to be creative with this drill and to play both offensive and defensive positions.

1. Set up group A at one side of the red line along the boards. Group B sets up opposite across the floor. Group C is next to group B, on the opposite side of the red line. Group D is opposite groups A and C on the red line. Group E is on the same side as group A at the blue line. Player F is on the same side as A in the center circle, player G is in the center circle opposite F, and player H is along the boards at the blue line on the same side as group C.

2. Play begins when F skates backward and receives a pass from A. Player B swings behind or in front of F, picks up a pass, and carries the puck down the opposite side of the floor. Player A also skates behind F to the opposite side to complete the two-player offense. They skate to the opposite goal with player G waiting on defense.

3. Player A then moves to queue D and vice versa, B moves to C and vice versa, G moves to H and vice versa, and F moves to E and vice versa.

The same play begins simultaneously at the other side of the floor. Player D passes to defensive player G, who passes to C, who breaks to the opposite goal with D against player F on defense.

Communication is vital in this drill. Encourage players to talk to each other and to be aware of who is on their team. Players will also need to keep their heads up while puck-handling to avoid collisions and to pick up passes.

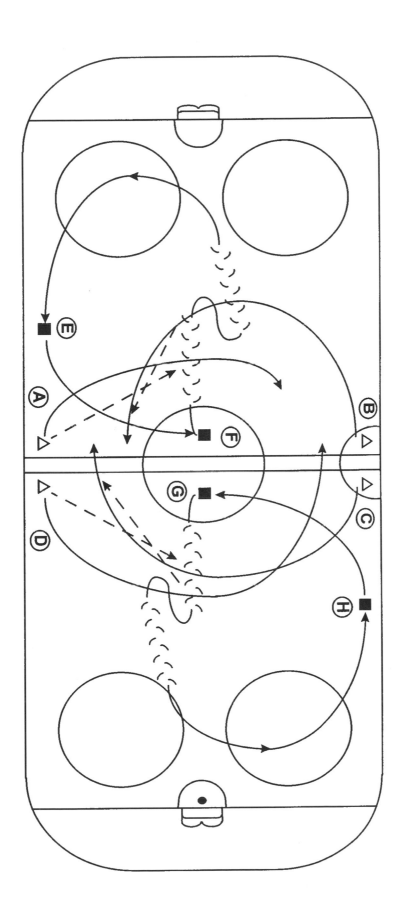

Key

△
Cone

○ ✕
Players
(offensive,
defensive)

■
Coach(es)

- - - - - - - -
Passing (or
the path of
the puck)

〰〰〰
Backward
skating

→
Forward
skating

═══
Hockey Stop

Figure 8.10
**Intermediate
Drill #4**

Intermediate Drill #5

This is a progressive drill that creates a three-on-one situation and where all players start simultaneously. It encourages good shooting, seeing and using the whole floor, and reading the play. It can be used as a quick break exercise that stresses good passing and defensive execution.

1. Set up groups A, B, C, and D on the four inside corners of the blue line. Groups A and B are on one side of the floor, groups C and D are opposite. Group D is primarily a defense line, although all of the players can be rotated through the different positions.
2. Player A takes a shot on the goal closest to the circle, then turns to the corner and picks up a puck (or receives a pass from the coach).
3. Players B and C start together. Player B skates between the circles and takes a shot on goal, turns to the boards and skates to the other goal. Player C skates down the floor, staying close to the boards and shoots on the goal from the face-off markings deep in the attacking zone. Since the players are shooting from different distances, these shots should be staggered enough for the goalie to react to each one.
4. The three-on-one commences with players B and C on the wing and player A in the center. After picking up the puck, A passes to C, who passes to B. Player D skates forward to the center and steps out to skate backward to defend against the three forwards.

To rotate the lines, have A move to B, B to C, C to D, and D to A.

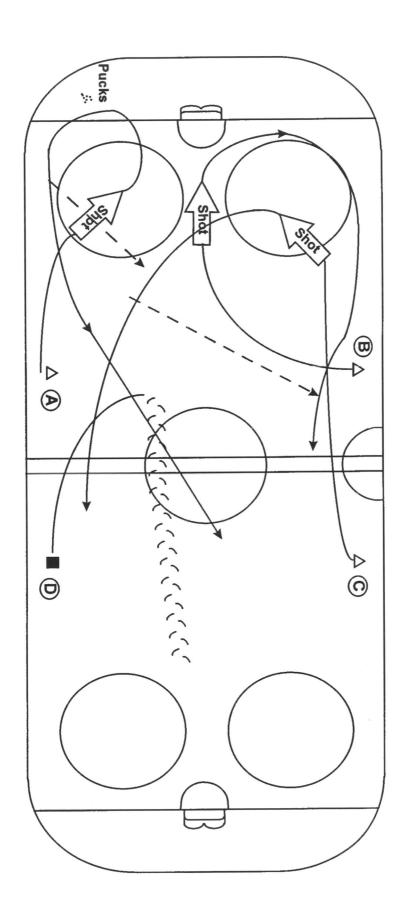

Key

△
Cone

○ ✕
Players
(offensive,
defensive)

■
Coach(es)

Passing (or
the path of
the puck)

◟◝◟◝
Backward
skating

→
Forward
skating

══
Hockey Stop

Figure 8.11
**Intermediate
Drill #5**

9

Team Play and Strategy

Team strategy is simply a plan to take advantage of the strengths and weaknesses of the opposing team. When developing a strategy, coaches should strive to ensure that both strengths and weaknesses of both their own team and the opposition are considered. In order for coaches to accomplish effective strategies, there must be two-way communication between players and coaches. What follows is a systematic approach to developing team strategy.

This system incorporates all players on the team into patterns of play which can then be applied in game situations and assessed for their effectiveness. Within this system, the coach must clearly define each player's role. This eliminates confusion and reduces the risk of an error during play.

The structured environment of the system gives weaker players an opportunity to help the team. Clearly defined roles also help boost the self-esteem of the weaker players and make it easier for them to contribute to the team effort.

■ OFFENSIVE STRATEGY

Offensive strategy involves systematic plays with flexibility designed to gain advantage over the opposition's defense. These plays can be used in both the defensive and offensive zones.

In the Defensive Zone

Breakouts

Breakouts are planned plays for moving out of the defensive zone into the offensive zone. A breakout normally begins with a defensive player and consists of one or more passes before leaving the defensive zone. Breakout patterns are especially important when the team is under pressure. It is good hockey strategy to include three or more breakout plays in your system.

1. A basic breakout play begins with a defender behind the net. One forward curls to or steps out to the boards on either side of the net for a pass, then passes to the second forward who breaks up near center floor.
2. The second defender waits near the net, maneuvering to stay open as an outlet for a pass, until the defender with the puck has passed to the forward. Once the pass has been successfully completed, the second defender breaks down the floor along the boards. One of the two defensive players always trails behind the break out in case the opposing team gets control of the puck.

Once players become comfortable with this basic breakout, it can be modified so that options are available for different situations.

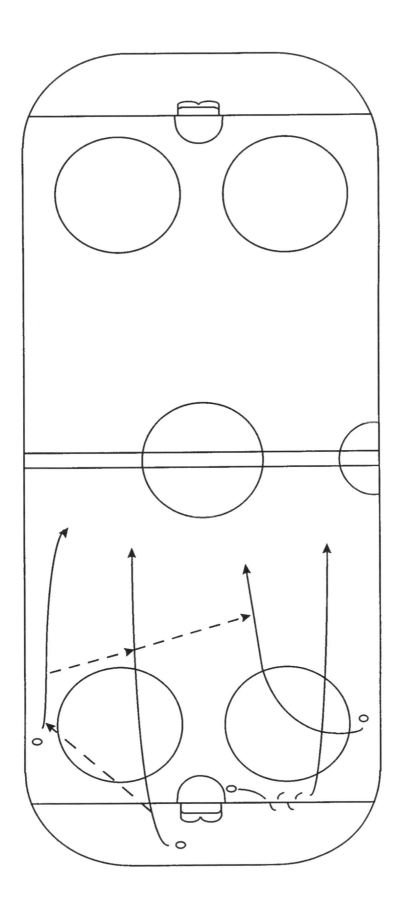

Key

△
Cone

○ ✕
Players
(offensive,
defensive)

■
Coach(es)

- - - - - - - -
Passing (or
the path of
the puck)

ᒼᒼᒼᒼ
Backward
skating

──────▶
Forward
skating

══
Hockey Stop

Figure 9.1
Breakout

9

Fast Breaks

Fast breaks usually begin when a defensive player on the opposing team makes a long, hard pass which is intercepted. Fast breaks are transition plays and, if successfully executed, catch the opposing team trapped in the defensive or neutral zone. These plays frequently result in great scoring opportunities.

In a basic fast break, the opposing team (marked with x's) attempts to clear the puck. This pass is intercepted by a player who then passes to a teammate breaking to the center, who in turn passes to another teammate breaking toward the opening in front of the net.

It is the quick movement of the intercepted puck that may catch the opposing team off guard or in the middle of a line change. Players must quickly reorient to the change from defense to offense to take advantage of a possible good scoring opportunity.

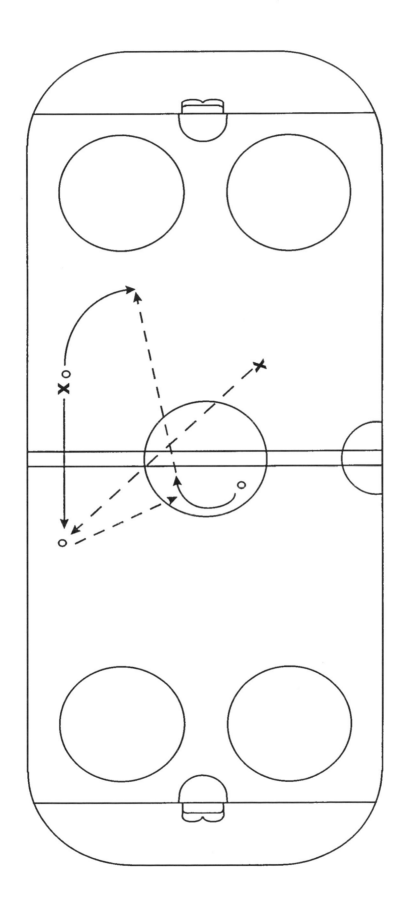

Key

△
Cone

○ ✕
Players
(offensive,
defensive)

■
Coach(es)

Passing (or
the path of
the puck)

︵︵︵
Backward
skating

⟶
Forward
skating

═
Hockey Stop

Figure 9.2
Fast break

Regrouping

When the defense has the puck in the defensive zone, they must control the puck while the forwards quickly reposition themselves. The forwards regroup by circling and accelerating up the playing surface. The defensive players then pass to the forwards as they move into the offensive zone.

In a basic regrouping situation, a wing passes back to a defender who skates backward and passes across to the second defender. On receiving the pass, the second defender skates forward to the center circle and passes to the wing, who has circled and accelerated to the other side of the playing area. The first wing loops around to center and to the far side. At this point, the wings have traded sides and the defenders trail them for the offensive attack.

Key

△
Cone

○✕
Players
(offensive,
defensive)

■
Coach(es)

Passing (or
the path of
the puck)

⌒⌒⌒
Backward
skating

→
Forward
skating

＝
Hockey Stop

Figure 9.3
Regrouping

In the Offensive Zone

Forechecking

Forechecking occurs when the first one or two players race into the offensive zone to force a turnover, eliminate options, or retrieve a loose puck. When properly executed, the opposition has insufficient time to set up and make a good play.

In this example of forechecking, the opposing team (marked with x's) is attempting to break out. The forechecking team is marked with o's. To practice the play, the coach sends a pass around the boards, where one player will attempt to recover the puck. Players who are forechecking immediately skate to positions just behind the opposing players to take away their space and attempt to steal any passes. The forechecking players always position themselves between their net and the opposing player. If executed correctly, this will cause the breakout team to turn over the puck.

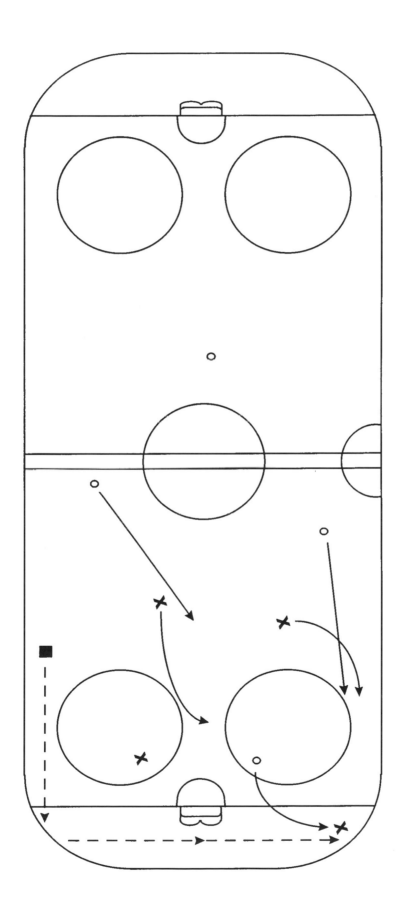

Key

△
Cone

○ ✕
Players
(offensive,
defensive)

■
Coach(es)

Passing (or
the path of
the puck)

ﹾﹾﹾﹾ
Backward
skating

⟶
Forward
skating

═══
Hockey Stop

Figure 9.4
Forechecking

Dump

A dump is a play that occurs when a team throws the puck deep into the opposing zone. This can happen in four situations: during line changes when players are tired, during planned plays when the team is in good position to retrieve the puck, during broken plays when the puck is dumped as an escape valve, and when penalty killing to clear the puck.

Two-on-One

In this situation, two offensive players manuever around one defensive player. Effective communication is necessary for the execution of this play. Give-and-go passes should be short and crisp to eliminate the risk of losing the puck. The two plays shown in figure 9.5 can be practiced at the same time at opposite ends of the floor.

In the play on the right, offensive player A starts with the puck and indicates that he or she is going to the net to draw the defensive player and the goalie. Player A then either shoots or passes to player B, who has skated into the slot. If player A passes to B, A should drive to the net for a tip in, play for a rebound, or screen the goalie.

In the play on the left, player A carries the puck toward the defensive player, sets a trap, and drops the puck to player B, who has skated in behind. Player B then accelerates to the net. Player A rolls to the inside and drives to the net to create an additional option for player B. Note that while creating the trap, little or no contact is made with the defensive player.

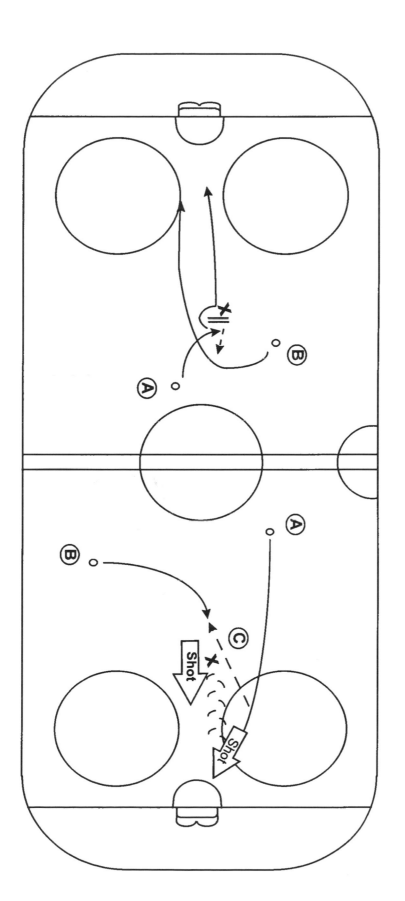

Key

△
Cone

○ ✕
Players
(offensive,
defensive)

■
Coach(es)

Passing (or
the path of
the puck)

〰️
Backward
skating

→
Forward
skating

═
Hockey Stop

Figure 9.5
**Two-on-one
plays**

Three-on-two

In this situation, three offensive players attack the two defenders. Communication and teamwork is even more critical in the three-on-two. Two-on-one and three-on-two plays should always result in a good scoring opportunity, or at least a shot on goal.

To practice this play, the three offensive team members start at the center line. The center passes to a wing. The wing carries the puck to the circle and either shoots or passes to the other wing who has skated into the slot. Meanwhile, the center skates directly to the goal. From this position, the center can screen the goalie, drawing one of the opposing players and leaving the trailer open in the slot, while a teammate shoots, receives a pass, or recovers a deflected shot.

In a three-on-two, the forwards, especially the one in position to shoot, must be ready to hurry back if the opposing team gets control of the puck. All three players should never be caught deep in the offensive zone.

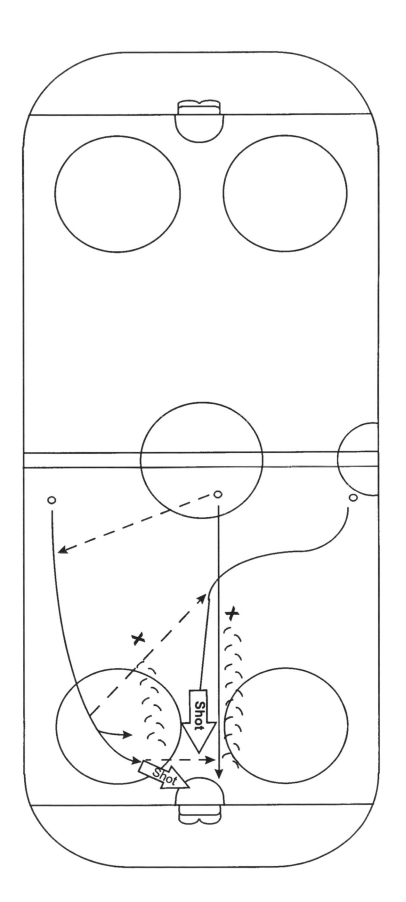

Key

△
Cone

○ ✕
Players
(offensive,
defensive)

■
Coach(es)

- - - - - - - -
Passing (or
the path of
the puck)

⌒⌒⌒⌒
Backward
skating

⟶
Forward
skating

═══
Hockey Stop

Figure 9.6
**Three-on-two
play**

9

Cycle and Flow

Cycle and flow generally refers to the systematic rotation of players within a small area of the offensive zone, but it is not limited to this zone and should be utilized anywhere on the playing surface when necessary. Rotation helps the team maintain control of the puck and open up scoring opportunities.

In this play, player A begins with the puck behind the net, player B lines up along the blue line, player C starts in the slot, and player D begins along the blue line opposite B.

Players A and B skate toward each other. Player A bounces a pass off the boards behind to player B. Player B catches the pass, turns in the corner, and passes to either A or

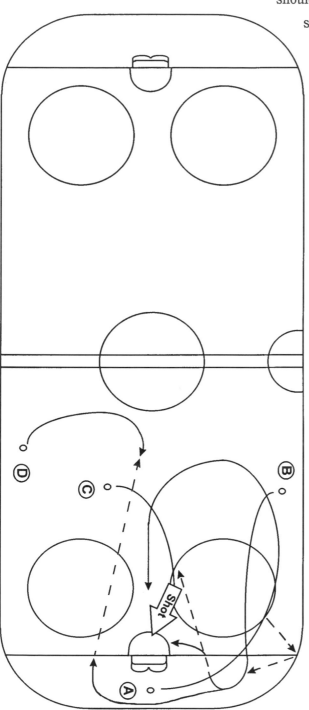

Figure 9.7a
Cycle and flow

C for the shot. If the pass goes to C, A follows for a rebound or tip-in. If the pass goes to A, player C screens the goalkeeper. If players A and C are not open, player B passes to player D, who shoots on net while two players among players A, B, and C screen the goalie. The free player gets ready to assume a defensive role should it become necessary.

If there is no shot, player C rotates to the position behind the net, Player B moves into the slot, and player A circles out to the boards. Repeat the rotation until a good shot opens up. In practice, have the players rotate through this cycle several times before they take a shot so they can get used to how the rotation feels.

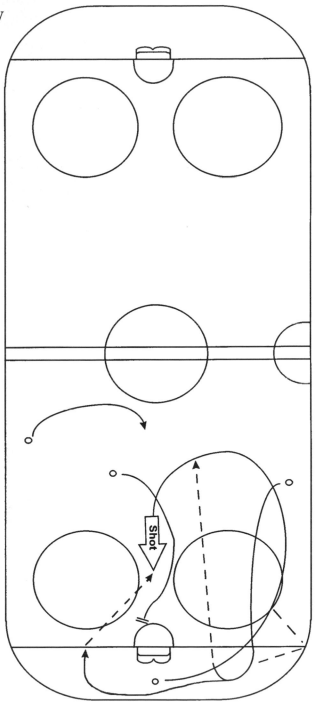

Figure 9.7b
Cycle and flow

Pinch

This somewhat risky move occurs when a defensive player moves ahead out of the usual defensive position to keep the puck in the offensive zone.

This play starts with a defender behind the net who tries to clear the puck along the boards. The second defender starts inside the circle and heads toward the boards. The opposing player starts at the top of the circle and forechecks the defender. The forechecker will have to act aggressively to gain control of the puck. The forechecking player must check out the surroundings and compute the odds of the play being successful before committing.

Offensive Strategy

In the defensive zone
- Breakouts
- Fast breaks
- Regrouping

In the offensive zone
- Forechecking
- Dump
- Two-on-one
- Cycle and flow
- Pinch

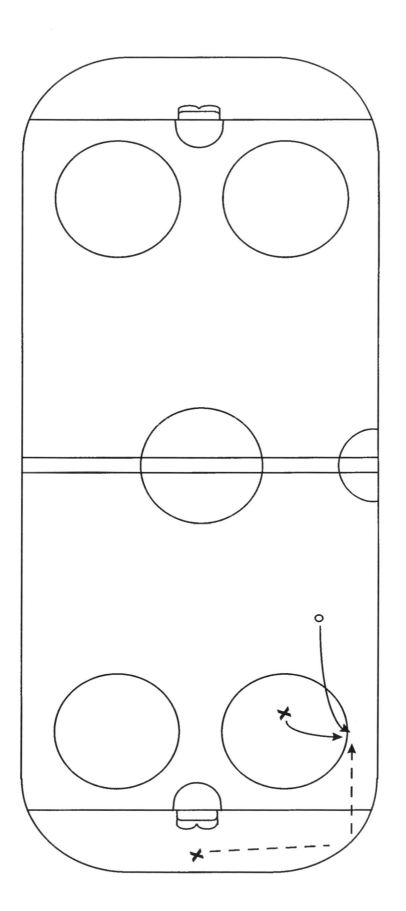

Key

△
Cone

○ ✕
Players
(offensive,
defensive)

■
Coach(es)

- - - - - - - -
Passing (or
the path of
the puck)

〵〵〵〵
Backward
skating

⟶
Forward
skating

══
Hockey Stop

Figure 9.8
Pinch

■ DEFENSIVE STRATEGY

Backchecking

Backchecking occurs when players quickly skate out of their offensive zone back to the defensive zone to help defend their goal as a result of having lost control of the puck.

Traps

Traps are a system used to maintain and protect a scoring lead. Four players wait in the neutral zone to prevent the other team from attempting a fast break or man-advantage rushes.

In this play, four players from the team on the defense start around the center circle. Three of them skate to where the puck goes. One player remains back slightly in case the opposing team is able to clear the puck. Four players from the team on the offense set up in their defensive zone with the puck and attempt to get it out of the zone.

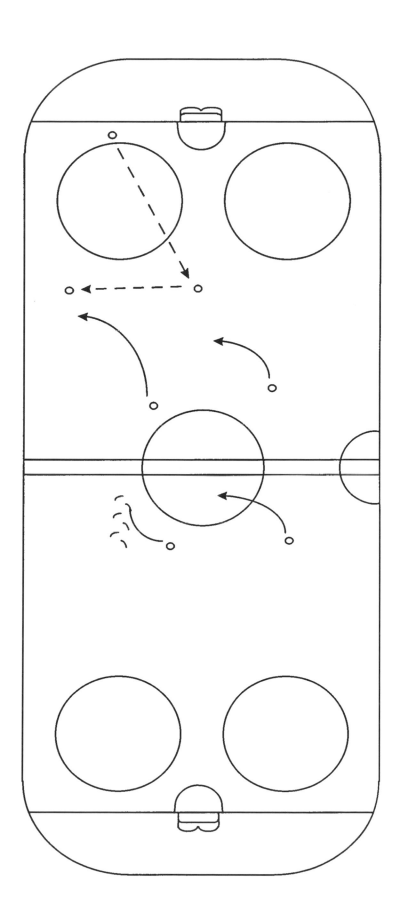

Key

△
Cone

○✕
Players
(offensive,
defensive)

■
Coach(es)

- - - - - - - -
Passing (or
the path of
the puck)

﹨﹨﹨﹨
Backward
skating

⟶
Forward
skating

═══
Hockey Stop

Figure 9.9
Traps

Zone Defense

This defense is a defensive system in which the defensive zone is split into four areas. Each player is then responsible for the defense of a designated area. This means that one defensive player may have to watch two players at once. Communication with teammates is vital to making this defense work.

In practicing a zone defense, demonstrate where the four defensive areas are. Set up four offensive players and four defensive players. The offensive players pass the puck to each other and occasionally drive to the net or try to fake the defense. The defensive players position themselves between the net and their respective opposing players without turning their backs on the play. In practice, the defensive players first concentrate on covering their zones. After they become adept at covering their zones, they make attempts to steal the puck from the offense.

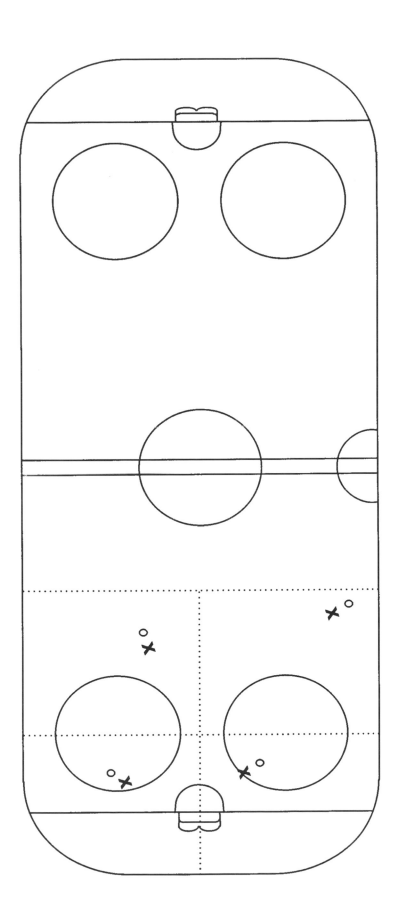

Figure 9.10
Zone defense

Man-to-Man

In this system, each player on the team on defense covers a player on the offensive team instead of covering a designated area. This is widely used in three-on-three situations. Although this system has gained some popularity, it is only effective when the defensive players communicate well with one another.

Defending Two-on-One Breaks

On two-on-one breaks, the defender must stay between the two attackers in an effort to push the puck to the outside. This serves two purposes. It gives the goaltender a one-on-one situation with the shooter, and it gives the defensive player an opportunity to take away the pass.

As the two offensive players attack with the puck, the defensive player tries to force the puck carrier wide without losing position between the attacking players and the net. The defensive player tries to make the puck carrier shoot from the outside or take away a pass made to the other offensive player.

If the offensive players set up a weave, the defensive player should continue to hold position between the two offensive players and the net. The defensive player should not commit to one player or the other and should let the goalie play the shooter from the angle.

Defensive Strategy
- Backchecking
- Traps
- Zones
- Man-to-man

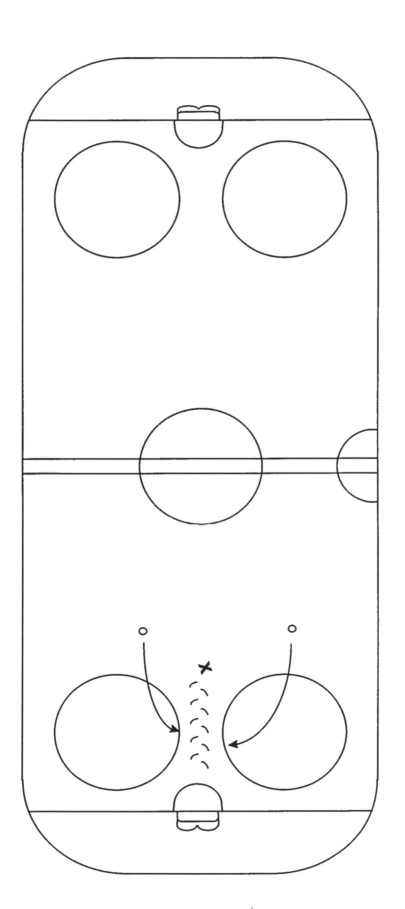

Figure 9.11
**Defending
against a
two-on-one**

■ GOALTENDING STRATEGY

Goaltenders have responsibilities unlike any other player on the team. This frequently puts them in the limelight where everyone watches their every move. Because goalies have this added pressure, many coaches feel they do better with some additional attention and respect. It is important that either the head coach or an assistant spend individual time with all the goalies, both starters and backups, at every practice.

Special Drills for Goalies

Each practice must include some drills designed specifically for goaltenders. Always discuss these with the goalies and incorporate their input whenever possible.

Game Breakdowns

Goalies play a psychologically vulnerable position and can become demoralized by a devastating period. One strategy coaches can use is to to treat each period as a mini-game. This helps the goaltender start fresh every period, mentally setting aside the mistakes and difficulties of previous periods.

Rotation

When there are two or more goalies on a team, a rotation system should be set up. One variation involves rotating them every other game; this tends to encourage a positive self-image. Goalies can also be rotated by period, thus sharing the pressures of each game. Each coach must decide which system works best for the team. As the season progresses, the system can be changed after assessing individual performances of goalies.

Pulling the Goalie for Poor Performance

An alternative to a rotation system is to play the hot goaltender until his or her play becomes inconsistent. If a goalie gives up a number of easy goals during a period, it may have a negative psychological impact on the rest of the team. A coach may wish to change goalies in that situation. If you take such action, you should always have a private talk with the goaltender who has been pulled to help bolster his or her confidence and maintain focus.

Pulling the Goalie at the End of Game

Some coaches choose to pull their goalie in the last two minutes of the final period when they are down by a goal and want an additional skater to provide an offensive threat. This strategy increases the team's chances of scoring a tying goal.

Goaltending Strategy

- Psychological support
- Special drills
- Game breakdowns
- Rotation
- Pulling goalie at end of game

■ FACE-OFF STRATEGY

An important aspect of game strategy is defining players' responsibilities during a face-off. In designating duties, make it clear to all players that they should be ready to adjust and react to any alignment changes made by the opposition.

It is always a good idea to have two players with strong face-off skills on the playing surface during critical face-off situations. There are times when the first player is ejected from the face-off by the referee due to a rule infraction or moving violation.

Face-off situations should be included in all practice sessions. They can come at the end of the session after practice time has been distributed according to the importance of other elements or skills.

Responsibilities of Face-off Players

Before moving to the face-off position, the face-off player ensures that the team is ready, based on how both teams line up.

Face-off players can use several strategies to win the face-off. First, they can use speed and quickness to hit the puck first and send it in the planned direction. Second, they can attempt to overpower their opponent by gripping lower on the shaft of the stick for added strength. They also can fake the direction of their draw using a forehand or backhand, as determined by their location on the playing surface, to confuse their opponent.

At times during a game (such as during a penalty killing in the defensive zone, at the end of the game, especially a tie game), it is important to win face-offs. In these situations, the face-off player should ignore the puck and go for the opponent's stick. This will allow teammates to take control of the puck. If face-off players cannot use their sticks and the puck remains in their vicinity, they can use a quick kick to send the puck in the right direction.

■ POWER PLAY STRATEGY

It is strictly up to the coach to decide which players to use during power play. It is a good idea to use as many different players as possible to give everyone on the team a chance to play. However, a predefined group of players should be prepared for critical game situations.

Set-ups

The strategic positioning of players in the offensive zone is called a set-up. This gives the team a place to start their offensive power play.

When a team has an especially talented player, place that player in a defensive position to quarterback or control the power play, breakout, and set-up.

To practice a basic offensive power play strategy, set player A near the center of the blue line, player B at the top of the right circle, and player C against the boards. On the defensive team, one player is in the circle, the other two near the net.

Offensive player A skates into the circle and traps the defensive player there. Players B and C move around either side of the trapped defense. Player B, with puck, either shoots or passes to player C and screens the goalie. Player C either traps the defense near the net and screens the shot for player B, or receives a pass and shoots.

Man-in-Front

On power plays, there should always be a player positioned in front of the opposing goalie to act as a screen, deflect the puck, and collect rebounds.

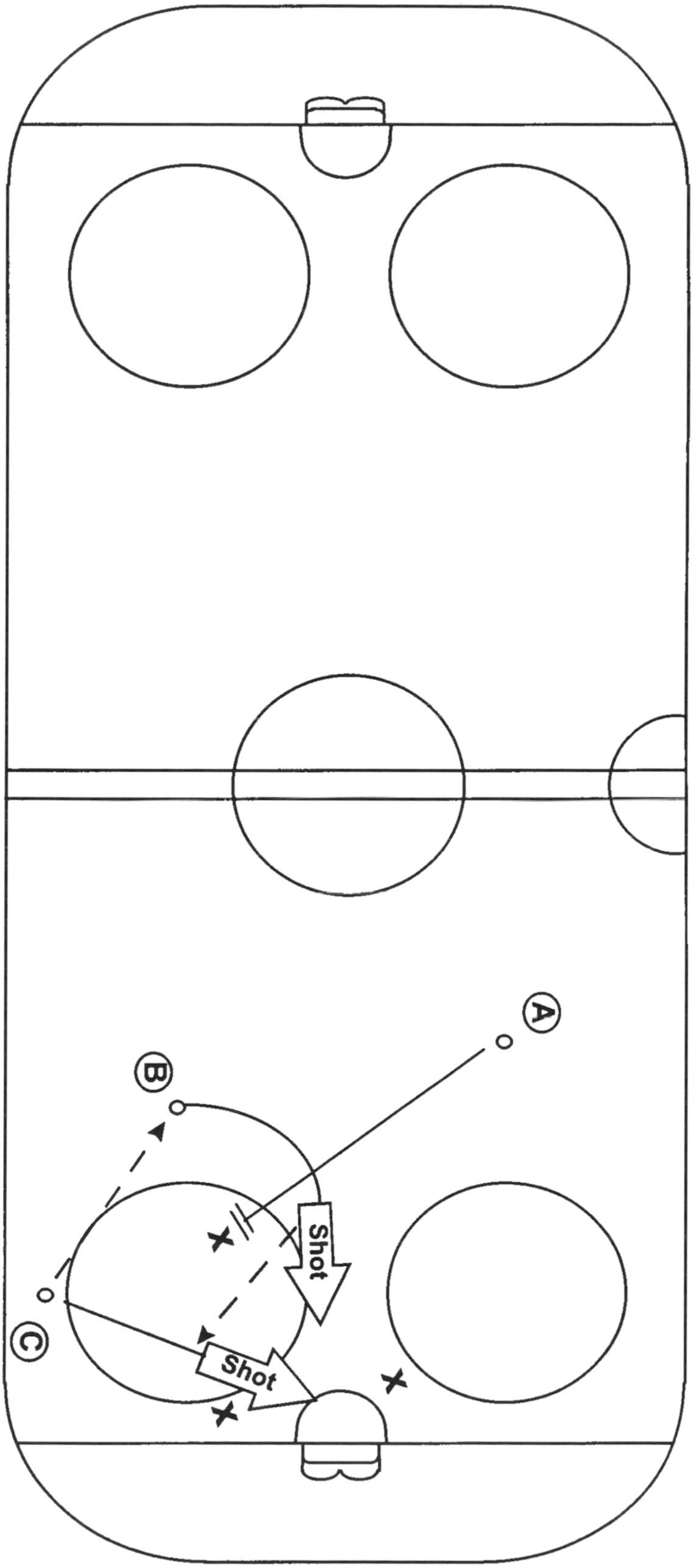

Key

△
Cone

○✕
Players (offensive, defensive)

■
Coach(es)

Passing (or the path of the puck)

Backward skating

Forward skating

Hockey Stop

Figure 9.12
Set-ups

■ PENALTY KILLING STRATEGY

As with power plays, the coach must decide which players to use during penalty killing time. It is a good idea to use as many different players as possible to spread around playing time, but a predefined group, however, will be wanted for critical game situations.

One strategy for defending shorthanded is the rotating triangle. Two defenders set up close to the net while the third stays high. One of the low defenders skates across to the other defender, who moves up to the high position and sends the defender at the top to a lower position. As the puck moves, the players rotate in this way to prevent the opposing team from getting into the slot.

An example, shown in figure 9.13b, shows what happens if a pass goes behind the net. The offensive team has many opportunities to move into the slot. However, the defensive team can rotate into position and limit the offense's options.

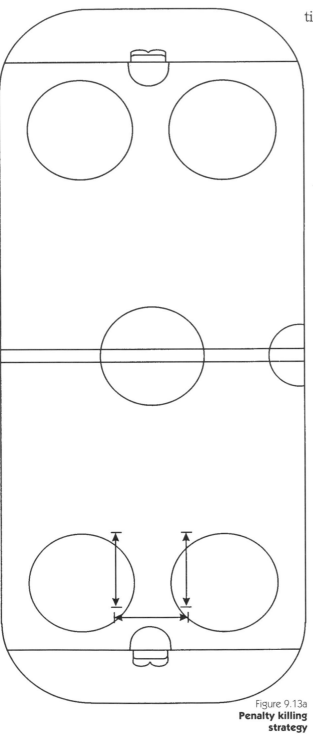

Figure 9.13a
**Penalty killing
strategy**

Discipline

Plays chosen for penalty killing should be predefined, practiced regularly, and carried out in a manner disciplined in the game. This is not the time for players to show initiative. Players out of position on this type of move can be counter-productive and can lead to a scoring oppotunity for the opponent.

Offensive Breaks

Although a team should concentrate on defensive strategy during penalty killing, players should be ready to react and take advantage of any offensive opportunities that arise.

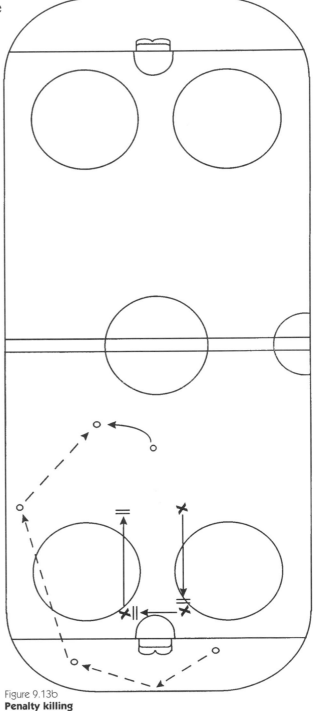

Figure 9.13b
Penalty killing strategy

Face-off, Power Play, and Penalty Killing Strategies

- Responsibilities of face-off man
- Speed and quickness
- Power
- Faking of draw
- Stick checking
- Kicking the puck
- Back-up face-off player in critical situations
- Use as many different players as possible
- Breakouts
- Set-ups
- Quarterbacks
- Man in front

■ LINE CHANGES DURING PLAY

It is vital that everyone on the team understand the quickest and most efficient way to execute line changes. During the game, it is important that the coach let the next line know well in advance of any line change. This gives the players time to prepare for the change.

Practice line changes early in the season and include them in practice from time to time as the season progresses, particularly if the team is having difficulty with smooth transitions during a game.

■ TIME OUTS DURING A GAME

Time outs can be used at any time during the game and can help the team regroup and concentrate on the game strategy as worked on in practice.

■ STATISTICS

Statistical data make it easier to evaluate the performance of both the team and individual players. Bear in mind, however, that statistics are only statistics; they never tell the whole story of what is happening in game situations.

An analysis of game statistics should include:

• The number of shots and shot location taken by both teams.
• The number of goals and assists made by each player and the team as a whole.
• The number of team and individual penalty minutes.
• The players on the floor for all even-strength goals.
• The number of team and individual giveaways.

These facts can help the coach determine how individual players mesh with each other as a team. Team statistics also can be used to determine the best face-off players (the coach should always know who is the best face-off player on the playing surface). Goalie statistics can also be calculated from team statistics. Since defensive play is a team effort, coaches should emphasize that goalie statistics are really a team statistic rather than an individual one.

Coaches should also keep adequate statistics on the opponents.

Evaluating how the teams matched up in previous meetings helps when planning strategy for future games against the same team. Coaches should evaluate the performance of both individuals and the team after each game, with some time spent evaluating the opposition's performance.

Attendance

Coaches should keep track of attendance, both for practice and games. Players who have poor attendance records are generally poor team players and should be counseled about regular attendance.

10

Risk Management

Risk management is a process designed to assess and minimize risks. Accidents can occur anytime, anywhere, and to anyone. In a fast-paced sport such as in-line hockey, there is potential for serious injuries and lawsuits arising from those injuries.

Everyone in the in-line hockey program must be committed to athlete and spectator health and safety and should recognize that it is better to eliminate or cut back a program rather than expose participants to unsafe conditions.

This chapter, excerpted from the NIHA Risk Management Guide, will help coaches to recognize the basic concepts of risk management and to understand their role in making in-line hockey a safer game for all participants.

It is important to stress that unless the risk management activities outlined in this guide are effectively practiced, no insurance fund will be adequate to protect against such adverse risk exposure. Risk management is the first line of defense. Insurance is the last line.

■ SCOPE OF RISK MANAGEMENT

Risk management must be comprehensive, covering every aspect of injury risk. All athletes are at risk. Anytime an individual is physically active, especially in a comprehensive program, there is a possibility of trauma.

The coach should alert team players to all situations which may expose them to injury by explaining the causes and mechanisms of how injuries are most likely to occur. Coaches must make a reasonable effort to provide for the well-being of athletes. Window dressing will not protect the athletes or reduce chances of liability exposure. Risk management is not a one-time effort. It requires an ongoing commitment and repeated review.

■ KEY INGREDIENTS OF RISK MANAGEMENT

Safety Committee

Coaches can help select a specific group of people to conduct the risk management program. These people are responsible for identifying needed safety measures and ensuring their implementation. The committee should include representation from administration, referees, coaching, and sports medicine.

Advance Planning

Allow adequate time to implement safety measures, whether modifying or constructing facilities, hiring personnel, or setting up an emergency accident plan. Access available resource persons and apply principles of effective communication to identify all foreseeable risks.

Implement Program

It is not enough to simply plan. The coach must ensure that necessary safety measures are clear to everyone involved in the program and that they are implemented.

Preseason and Postseason Review

Before the season begins, the coach should review the risk management plan with the team. By distributing the plan in writing and practicing skills like first-aid and emergency situations, the team will be able to operate more safely from the start. After the season, discuss the program's effectiveness and implement any needed changes for the next season.

Common Sense

The most important guideline for increasing safety in an in-line hockey program is to apply the collective common sense of everyone involved.

Public Awareness

If spectators and parents are knowledgeable about the plan, they can help ensure the safe operation of the program.

■ SAFETY PRACTICES

Setting up a safety program for the team will help considerably in reducing the frequency and severity of accidents. The following points are essential to its success.

Staff

An appropriate coach/player ratio covering all areas of expertise is essential. Staff members must participate in continuing education to ensure required training and competence. They must also comply with the state's applicable laws and regulations regarding qualifications.

Facilities

The condition of the facility must reasonably ensure player and spectator safety. Regular inspection, maintenance, and defined procedures for dealing with hazards are essential.

Equipment

Equipment must be used as intended by the manufacturer, comply with established rules and standards, and provide necessary protection. Equipment must be fitted properly and regularly inspected. It is important to ensure that replacement items can be provided quickly during activity sessions. Damaged equipment should not be used by players.

Rules of the Game

Athletes must be taught correct sports-specific techniques for improving skills. They need a clear understanding of the rules of play, particularly relating to safety, and the role equipment plays in injury prevention. If players understand prevention, recognition, and care of injuries, they can guard themselves against unnecessary harm. They must also learn proper techniques of strength training and conditioning.

According to the NIHA rules, violence or intentional contact is strictly forbidden. This includes any deliberate body checking, cross checking, running or charging an opponent, or intentional "horsing around." Any intentional contact between players should be immediately addressed; players involved in the altercation should be prohibited from league play. It is important that league supervision detect and strive to avoid such incidences. If an incident occurs, an incident report should be filled out—even if no injury results.

Some examples of intentional contact forbidden under NIHA rules include: holding an opponent or his or her stick to impede play, tripping, highsticking, and impeding the course of the opponent—including one who does not have control of the puck/ball. Examples of technical violations which also are strictly prohibited include: using the stick in a way other than described by the rules of the game or throwing a stick in the direction of a puck/ball.

Many other actions are prohibited according to the NIHA Rules. It is the coach's responsibility to be familiar with such rules and to adequately enforce them.

Officiating

Coaches are responsible for ensuring competent officiating of NIHA in-line hockey activities. A common error is recruiting a volunteer to substitute for a trained or certified official. If league officials are not properly enforcing safety rules, coaches will be exposed to liability.

Safety Checklist

A detailed checklist is invaluable to facilitate inspections made at regular intervals and to ensure effective follow-up in correcting unsafe practices and playing conditions.

Safety Rules

At every facility, make sure safety rules pertaining to the behavior of patrons are prepared, posted in a conspicuous place, and rigidly enforced. Skating in a manner that endangers other skaters or interferes with their pleasure is strictly forbidden. Pushing, horseplay, and fighting should also be strictly forbidden.

Supervisors, officials, coaches, assistant coaches, and volunteers should be thoroughly familiar with the NIHA playing rules and the league's safety rules. They should be trained to recognize unsafe behavior and should follow league policy in coping with it. Safety rules and procedures must be continually enforced. Consistent application of rules and procedures in both competition and practice is necessary to ensure athlete compliance.

Player Informed Consent/Waivers

Legal requirements of risk warning and informed consent apply to all athletes in all programs. In addition, parental consent is required for minor athletes. The NIHA Player Registration & Waiver form has been specifically designed and approved by an insurance underwriter to comply with such legal requirements. Before allowing team members to play, it is imperative that the coach have each player (and player's parent or guardian if a minor) complete and sign the NIHA Waiver. Failure to do so may result in forfeiture of insurance benefits.

Because of the potential speed on in-line skates, it is essential that safety be the foremost concern of all those involved in the sport. There are several factors which further impact the potential danger of in-line hockey; unlike ice hockey, in-line hockey can be played outdoors in the summertime when there is a temptation for players to wear as little clothing as possible. This means that league managers, coaches, and parents alike must maintain vigilance, insisting that kids wear all required safety gear to guard against injury.

Protective Gear Requirements

Head injuries are the most serious injuries that one can endure. There are numerous injuries which are serious or permanent, which can be prevented by wearing a hockey helmet and full face cage. The front teeth are highly vulnerable to flying pucks, misplaced sticks, elbows, and shoulders. Wearing a mouthpiece protects the teeth, as well as gums, and provides shock absorption to avoid the possibility of concussion. Fingers and hands can become blistered and fractured if left unprotected. Therefore, it is essential that all players wear hockey gloves for stickhandling. Falling on pavement can result in serious cuts and abrasions. Players should wear clothing that does not leave any area of the body exposed and must wear knee, shin, and elbow pads to help buffer a fall.

In addition, goalies are highly vulnerable to impact from flying pucks. A puck to the chest can cause severe injury including heart attacks and sudden death. Therefore, it is imperative that all goalies wear chest padding.

Players eighteen years of age or over are required by NIHA rules to wear the following protective gear:

- Hockey helmet with strap
- Knee, shin, and elbow pads
- Hockey gloves
- Mouthpiece
- Protective cup
- Eye protection*

Players under eighteen years of age are required to wear the protective gear listed above along with a full-face cage or shield.

Goalies (regardless of age) are required to wear a chest and arm pads in addition to the above protective gear.

League managers and coaches should inspect and ensure that all players wear the above listed protective gear.

■ INSTRUCTION AND SUPERVISION

All sanctioned NIHA activities must be adequately supervised. Supervisors must be adequately trained (i.e., through coaches certification, clinics) and the number of supervisors present must be adequate to control usage/practices.

NIHA general liability insurance covers "supervised, sanctioned NIHA activities." As a coach, it is imperative that a program is developed in which adequate supervision is consistently maintained.

Coaching Certification

All coaches involved in NIHA leagues should be trained and qualified. The coach is a fundamental source of playing techniques, good sportsmanship, and application of game rules for players. The coach's status as a role model will directly impact players' attitudes and actions. Coaches should have some background and training to enable them to confront the many situations involved in youth sports leagues. The NIHA, through its affiliation with the NYSCA, provides training and certification for coaches working with youth in-line players. Coaches' certification clinics are offered throughout the country; contact the NYSCA at 1-800-729-2057 for clinic dates and locations.

*Strongly recommended

■ MAINTENANCE

Good housekeeping practices are essential to maintain the in-line hockey site and rink area in safe, clean condition. Although sites may have hazards common to most places of public assembly, the use of in-line skates creates special problems.

Site Surface

For both safety and the enjoyment of players, maintaining the playing surface in good condition and patrolling the surface for objects is a major responsibility of the league manager. Poor condition of the surface is a potential allegation in lawsuits stemming from in-line hockey accidents.

A good surface is smooth; it's not rough, covered with dirt, loose gravel, or litter. To keep the surface free of debris and litter, strict rules forbidding eating, drinking, and smoking on the rink should be passed and enforced. League managers and officials should patrol constantly for items on the surface and should remove them as soon as they are observed.

In outdoor facilities especially, league managers have to cope with the problem of dirt and bad weather conditions. In inclement weather (rain, snow, fog, etc.) league play should be immediately stopped and postponed until the weather conditions dissipate.

Inspecting the rink surface for holes and ruts and filling them promptly also is an important measure for the league manager to take. Holes and ruts in the surface can present unnecessary hazards.

To cope with the effects of bad weather conditions and damage to asphalt surfaces at outdoor facilities, resurfacing the play site may be necessary to maintain a smooth, safe playing surface.

Obstructions

If the site has any kind of obstruction nearby, precautions must be taken to ensure that if a player needs to bail out of the playing zone, he or she can do so safely. For example, if a permanent wall structure surrounds the site, it should be padded to protect a player crashing into it. Likewise, a light pole or basketball hoop pole should be covered with padding to guard against injuries to a player crashing into it.

If spectators are permitted to view in-line hockey games, care should be taken to avoid flying pucks from exiting the playing surface and potentially injuring a spectator. The most common, effective safety measure is the installation of protective netting surrounding the site.

Keeping a log

A log and other written records should be kept with respect to maintenance and other activities. These records will be particularly valuable if an incident occurs, a claim is made, and testimony has to be given in court. A log of cleaning and maintenance work kept by caretaking personnel might be used to show the efforts made to keep the site in good condition with hazards eliminated or adequately addressed for participant safety.

Since in-line hockey has inherent hazards that are completely beyond the control of the coaching staff, accidents will occur despite the most careful preventative measures. The coach, therefore, should set up a plan for handling accidents and injuries as effectively as possible and should see that his or her staff and volunteers are thoroughly familiar with the procedure.

The telephone numbers of a nearby doctor, an ambulance service or rescue squad, and a nearby hospital should be posted, and all personnel and volunteers should be familiar with its location.

■ NEGLIGENCE

More inclusive information for coaches on negligence and sports-related lawsuits is included in the NIHA Risk Management Guide.

Coaches should be aware that in sports-related lawsuits, the most frequent legal claim raised is based on the laws of negligence. Negligence is often described as doing something which an ordinary, prudent person would not have done under similar circumstances or failing to do something which an ordinary, prudent person would have done under similar circumstances.

Where an injured person believes that his or her injuries were caused by the negligence of someone else, he or she has the right to commence a lawsuit claiming an amount of money for financial loss, pain, and suffering from the allegedly negligent person.

Elements of Negligence

In an action for negligence, the plaintiff must show that the defendant owed the plaintiff a duty, that there was a negligent act or omission by the defendant, that there is casual connection between the defendant's action or lack of action and the injury, and that damages resulted from the defendant's action (or inaction). Negligence is measured on a case-by-case basis, taking into account all the facts and circumstances present.

A coach in an in-line hockey league must conform to the standard of care of a reasonable, prudent person. Ordinary is not enough. Participants and spectators in the league must at all times be protected from undue risk of harm by the way the in-line hockey program is conducted and by the playing surface conditions.

In-line hockey players are not immune from potential liability for negligence. Deliberate fighting, cheap shots, rough housing, showing off or fooling around which results in the injury of other players or spectators will lead to legal liability. Coaches, officials, and others who encourage or condone such actions might also be held responsible for any resulting injury. All participants should attempt to ensure that in-line hockey is played cleanly and fairly and that dangerous activities are not part of the game.

The NIHA strongly suggests the use of checklists to assist in decreasing potential liability for negligent acts or omissions. The league organizer and coaches must aggressively answer the question, "Are all foreseeable areas of risks" legally responded to? The league should stress warnings, waivers, instruction, on-the-spot supervision, state-of-the-art equipment, strict adherence to all NIHA safety rules, well-trained, well-informed NYSCA certified coaches and NIHA certified referees, and a written and strictly enforced set of procedures, policies, and evaluations.

11

Injuries and First-Aid Treatment

Since injuries are inevitable, it is very important that coaches have a thorough understanding of their prevention and treatment. One way to obtain this information is through a course in Basic First Aid and CPR (Cardio-Pulmonary Resuscitation).

Below are suggestions of how to prevent, recognize, and treat injuries common to in-line hockey.

■ POINTS TO REMEMBER

Equipment

Players should only use equipment that has been designed to prevent injury and is approved by the HECC, CSA, or ATM.

Stretching and Physical Conditioning

A good stretching program focuses on flexibility and substantially can reduce the number of injuries over a season. Stretching should be done during both warm up and cooling off sessions. Players in good physical condition are less susceptible to injuries.

Water

Prevent dehydration by supplying players with ample water during games and practice.

Playing Surface Conditions

Coaches should always conduct a walking inspection of the playing surface before any practice or game to ensure the surface is safe for playing and inform players of any areas on the playing surface that may be rough or otherwise unsafe to skate on. They can then avoid these areas and reduce the risk of minor or serious injuries.

Enforcement of Rules

Rules are made to ensure the safety of all players, and it is important that games be played according to those rules. It is the responsibility of coaches and referees to enforce all rules to minimize the risk of injury to players.

Medicals

All players should undergo a thorough medical examination prior to beginning practice.

Injury Insurance

All coaches and players should obtain injury insurance in case of serious injury during the season.

First-Aid Kits

Each team should maintain a well-equipped first-aid kit. A list of supplies that should be included in this kit can be obtained from a certified first-aid instructor or first-aid supply company. Someone should be assigned to check the kit on a regular basis and replenish any needed supplies.

Parents

Coaches should report all injuries, no matter how small, to the parents of injured players. Parents should let the coaches know when the player is cleared to play again.

■ EMERGENCY PLAN

Although coaches rarely encounter true emergency situations, they should have a plan in place so that if an emergency does arise, everyone on the team, including players and coaching staff, are prepared to deal with it.

The plan should instruct everyone to remain calm, listen to any instructions, and take care of all assigned duties. One member of the coaching staff should maintain a record of the location of the arena or sport facility where the game is being played, the location of the nearest hospital, emergency phone numbers of ambulance, fire department, hospital, if there is no local 911 number, and the plan of action for an emergency. The following guidelines are exempted from the NIHA Risk Management Guide.

When an accident occurs, the injured person should not be moved until the manager or a qualified first aid professional gives approval. If the person appears to be seriously injured, an ambulance should be called so that a stretcher handled by trained attendants can be used to move the person safely. If a minor is injured, the manager should immediately phone the parents to inform them and to ask for instructions.

Proper treatment and sympathetic handling of an injured person can go a long way in removing any animosity the person may feel toward the rink, and thus reduces the possibility of a liability suit.

Attend to the injured player as soon as possible, but remain in control. Experience teaches that an all-out rush to assist an injured player causes the rescuer to be out of breath and unable to think clearly.

Do not move the injured player until an adequate assessment has determined that it is safe to move him or her. Do not hesitate to ask for assistance, or to call 911 if there is any question of the player's safety.

Approach the injured player in a calm, reassuring fashion (not always easy). Talk in a low voice, speak softly, and assuredly. Trust goes a long way; try not to do or say anything that will undermine that trust. Even if an injury appears to be very serious, it is important that the player remains calm so that the injury does not worsen.

Report all injuries, no matter how minor, to the player's parents. It is their decision when to refer their child to the family physician.

Examining the Injured Player

The first thing to do when arriving at the side of the injured player is to make an immediate assessment of the severity of the situation. This is done by looking for the most serious life-threatening problems first.

Handling an Unconscious Player

If the unconscious player is not breathing or has no pulse, remove the player's helmet and begin CPR. **DO NOT REMOVE THE HELMET UNLESS ABSOLUTELY NECESSARY.**

- Removing the helmet is potentially dangerous since there is no certain way to know if the unconscious player has had an injury to his or her neck.
- If available, use tools to cut the face mask off and leave the helmet in place; this will afford some more protection to the neck.
- If the helmet must be removed, delegate one person to stabilize the head and neck. Unsnap the chin straps, lift the face mask, and gently remove the helmet while supporting the neck. If possible, wait for emergency officials to arrive.
- Delegate someone to call 911 and post someone to direct the ambulance to the injured player.

If the unconscious player has a pulse and is breathing, **DO NOT REMOVE THE HELMET.** The player could have an injury to the neck; permanent paralysis could result from attempting to remove the helmet. Call 911 immediately, do not allow anyone to move the player's head, and monitor him or her carefully until the ambulance arrives.

Heat Illnesses

Since in-line hockey is played in all climates, players are susceptible to heat exhaustion and heat stroke. Common signs of heat exhaustion include fatigue, dizziness, nausea, restlessness, headache, and profuse sweating. The skin may be pale and clammy, breathing is fast and shallow, and the pulse is rapid and weak. Vomiting and/or fainting can occur.

Treatment

Transport the player into the shade if possible, begin cooling him or her with water, and remove playing equipment. If the athlete is conscious, let him or her drink cool water. Athletes suffering from heat exhaustion should be withdrawn from further activity for the remainder of that day and should seek medical attention. If heat exhaustion is not treated immediately, it can lead to heat stroke.

When a player has heat stroke, sweating often stops completely, the skin becomes hot, dry, and reddened, breathing is shallow and the pulse is rapid and weak. The body temperature can rise dramatically. Without treatment, the player may quickly lose consciousness and die.

The treatment for heat stroke entails reducing the body temperature quickly. Cool the player by placing ice cold towels around the body and sponging with cool water. Remove the clothing and equipment to prevent the retention of body heat. Allow the player to drink water only if he or she is conscious. Players with heat stroke are critically ill; call 911 and transport them to a medical facility.

Shock

This often occurs after a serious injury, but it may occur due to fear or emotional upset, bee or insect stings, or allergic reaction to foods. Signs of shock include a weak or rapid pulse; cold, clammy skin, heavy or difficult breathing, pale skin, weakness, and unconsciousness.

Once these potentially life-threatening injuries have been ruled out, begin assessing the condition of the injured player by asking questions. Sometimes the injured player will need to be calmed down before he or she can tell you what happened, or where it hurts.

- The first step in examination is to look at the player. Look for bleeding, bruising, or deformity that suggests a broken bone.
- The next step is to feel the injured area gently, looking for swelling or tenderness over bones that suggest a fracture.
- Next, have the player move the injured part carefully to see if he or she can do so without pain. If the player can, then it is safe to move the player from the rink. If the player cannot move without pain, it means there is the possibility of a more serious injury, and the player should not be moved until proper protection of the extremity (i.e., a splint) has been applied.
- If there is any question of a fracture to the leg, do not remove the player's skate, since more harm may be done by manipulating a broken leg.

Common Injuries and Their Treatment

Contusion or Bruise
- Usually caused by a blow from an object such as a hockey stick, ball, another player, or fall.

- Assess severity of injury. If the player is unable to move the injured part, suspect fracture and apply a splint, ice, and call 911 to transport to a medical facility.
- Contusions to certain areas can be life-threatening: heart and chest wall, spleen (upper left abdomen), kidney (flank), and should be referred to an emergency room or family physician.
- Contusions to other specific areas which may require medical attention include testicular injuries and injuries to the eyes and face.
- Most contusions are well treated with ice and mild supportive wrap to prevent swelling.

Laceration (Cut)

- Usually caused by a blow from an object such as a hockey stick, ball, another player, or fall.
- Whenever possible, use gloves and take precautions if there is contact with blood.
- Most bleeding can be controlled with a pressure dressing.
- Players must not participate with an open laceration or blood on any part of their uniform or equipment.
- Application of ice will help control bleeding and pain.
- Transport player to a medical facility for appropriate care.

Sprain

- A sprain represents tearing of ligaments around a joint and can be mild, moderate, or severe (a complete tear with dislocation from the joint).
- A sprain usually results from a twisting injury. A "pop" usually signifies a more serious injury.
- Assess the severity of the injury as mild, moderate, or severe.
- Use ice or crutches if required. Players with significant swelling, inability to walk without pain, or other signs of serious injury should be referred to their physician.

Fracture (Broken Bone)

- Fractures are either closed (skin intact) or open (skin broken).
- Obvious deformity or a bone that bends in an abnormal place is a sign of a serious injury.

- Other signs of fractures include immediate swelling and tenderness over the bone. Pain with movement of the extremity indicates a more severe injury, but a fracture can be present even if the player is able to move his or her arm or leg. The ability to move the fingers and toes is never an indication that a fracture is not present.
- Open fractures are true medical emergencies. Cover the wound with a sterile gauze pad if available, splint the extremity, and transport (by ambulance if necessary) to a hospital emergency room.
- Closed fractures should be splinted and transported.
- Applying ice to the fracture site will help control the swelling and pain.
- Injuries to the growth plates (at the end of bones) are common in children and can be mistaken for sprains. Any time the player has pain when attempting to move a joint, apply a splint, ice, and transport him or her to the appropriate medical facility.

Injuries to the Hands

- Usually caused by a direct blow from a fall, hockey stick, or ball.
- Assess for deformity, swelling, and tenderness.
- Ask the player to move the finger.
- "Buddy taping" a finger to an adjacent, noninjured finger will provide protection and relief.
- Apply ice to control swelling and pain.
- Refer player to his or her physician if the finger has significant deformity, even if it has been corrected.

Injuries to the Face

- Despite face guards, injuries to the face can occur.
- Look for bleeding from the nose, obvious shifting of the appearance of the face, and/or swelling. Examine for tenderness over the facial bones, and ask the player to move his or her jaws and eyes.
- For a nosebleed, use compression to the nostrils and apply ice.
- Transport the player for appropriate emergency care.

Injuries to the Teeth

- Injuries to the teeth are usually caused by a direct blow to the mouth.
- If a tooth is broken, try to find the broken piece to make sure the player has not aspirated it into his or her lungs.

- If the tooth has been completely knocked out, it must be replaced within one hour. Keep the tooth moist (milk is good if available) and do not handle it by the root.
- Refer the player to his or her dentist immediately.

Injuries to the Eyes

- Injuries to the eyes occur rarely. Proper care can make the difference between blindness and recovery.
- Assess the injury; ask the player about pain in the eye, doubled or blurred vision.
- Inspect the eye for unequal or uneven pupils, blood, cuts, and/or swelling.
- Ask the player to move the eyes and look for differences in the eyes.
- Cover the eye with an eye shield (or cut-off bottom of a cup) making sure to put no pressure on the eye.
- Transport the player to the appropriate medical facility.

• • •

It is essential that an accurate and complete report of every accident resulting in injury, regardless of how minor the injury is, be made at once. It is impossible to determine what type of incident might ultimately result in a claim being filed. A person can look perfectly normal, walk away, and then later on, for instance, claim limited motion in his or her shoulder.

If the incident is not reported at the time it occurs, the coach has no basis whatsoever for a defense. The use of such a report is admissible in court and will have the added advantage of impressing on the jury the fact that the coach has made accident control a regular part of team operations.

NIHA Infectious Diseases Guidelines

The NIHA publishes these guidelines in an effort to minimize the possibility of transmission of any infectious disease during in-line hockey practice or games.

These guidelines primarily address blood-borne pathogens such as the Hepatitis B virus and the HIV virus. All activity by the participants in

NIHA-sanctioned programs should be carried out with the safety of the participants in mind, in a safe, healthy environment.

Although these guidelines are not regulations, the NIHA strongly recommends that coaches in each local league adhere to and carry them out in the day-to-day operations of their teams. Coaches should be aware that it is most important to carry out suggested procedures in the interest of safety and the health of children who participate in team activities on a day-to-day basis.

Blood-Borne Pathogens

Blood-borne pathogens such as Hepatitis B and HIV are serious infectious diseases which are present in blood as well as other bodily fluids such as semen, vaginal fluids, and breast milk.

The precise risk of HIV transmission during exposure of open wounds or mucous membranes such as eyes, ears, nose, and mouth to contaminated blood is not known. However, evidence suggests that the risk is very low. In fact, the possibility of contracting HIV in this manner is much less than the possibility of contracting Hepatitis B and other blood-borne vital infections. One must not assume, however, that the chance of transmission of HIV in this manner is zero. Proper and adequate precautions should be taken to ensure that no transmission can occur.

Ways to Prevent the Transmission of Blood-Borne Pathogens

If blood is present, taking the following steps can lessen the possibility of a blood-borne pathogen if the person who is bleeding has an infectious disease.

If a player has an open wound on their body, he or she should cover this wound prior to the start of practice or a game. When this is done, the player will decrease the risk of transmission of a blood-borne pathogen from the open wound to another person.

When giving first-aid to others, an individual should wear protective gloves (such as rubber or surgical gloves) anytime blood, an open wound, or mucous membranes are involved. The individual should wear clean gloves for each person treated or when treating the same person more than one time.

If an individual gets someone else's blood on his or her skin, the blood should be wiped off with a disposable towel using a disinfectant such as isopropyl alcohol (rubbing alcohol). Protective gloves should be worn at all times.

If an individual begins to bleed during practice or a game, play must be stopped and the individual should be removed from the playing surface. If there is blood on the floor, the floor should be cleaned using a disinfectant solution of household bleach and water. The surface should then be rinsed with clean water to avoid participants getting the disinfectant in their eyes. The person doing this clean up should wear protective gloves.

The individual removed from practice or a game due to bleeding must have the bleeding stopped and any wound covered before he or she is allowed to return to the practice or the game. If the bleeding begins again, the practice or game should be stopped and the potentially contaminated surface cleaned. The coach or referee should judge the number of times the game should be stopped before the individual is disqualified from further participation in the practice session or the game.

The person who has treated an injury where there is blood present or has cleaned a potentially contaminated surface should wash their hands with soap and hot water, whether or not protective gloves are worn.

Disposable towels should be used in all clean up. Towels, gloves, and all protective materials used in the clean up, as well as items used to stop the bleeding, should be placed in a sealed container lined with a plastic bag. These bags are not to be reused and should be disposed of on a daily basis.

Other Contagions

Contagions such as the influenza virus, the common cold, and the mononucleosis virus are generally transmitted by respiratory secretions, saliva, and nasal discharge. This transmission occurs through the air when an infected person sneezes or coughs, or by oral inoculation from contaminated hands and surfaces. The possibility of becoming infected with one of these viruses is greater indoors than outdoors.

If a person is infected with one of these viruses, they possibly will have an incubation period of a few hours or days. Colds and influenza are usually known by the individual who may be affected and the normal symptoms include muscle aches, pains in the joints, fever, and chills. If an individual is affected, that player should not be allowed to practice or play in a game due to the weakness that would be present from these viruses. It is important to observe sound hygienic practices when this occurs, taking special care that towels, cups, and water bottles are not shared among participants.

■ WHEN AN INJURED PLAYER RETURNS

Players often try to return from an injury before they are fully recovered, so coaches should require medical clearance from a doctor before allowing a player to participate in practice or play in a game. This will help prevent unrecovered players from returning to the injury list.

12

Rules, Regulations, and Terms

Both coaches and players should have a thorough understanding of the NIHA rules and regulations. All coaches should know the rules and regulations contained in the NIHA Official Rule Book and carry a copy of the book with them during all practices and games so they can provide accurate information to their players. The rule book also can be referred to as a source for solving officiating dilemmas.

Although not an official part of the rules and regulations of in-line hockey play, coaches should teach teams to play with the utmost regard for sportsmanship and discipline. It is embarrassing to coaches, parents, other players, and bystanders when team members display unsportsmanlike conduct before, during, or after a game.

Players must know what they can and cannot do as they play the game or else they will be constantly questioning the coach about the rules. Team captains must be most knowledgeable about the rules since they are responsible for discussing the interpretation of them with the officials during games.

■ REFEREE SIGNALS

Players and coaches should have a thorough knowledge of the referee signals shown on the following pages.

HOLDING

Clasp wrist of whistle hand with the other hand well in front of the chest.

HOOKING

A series of tugging motions with both arms, as if pulling something toward the stomach.

INTERFERENCE

Crossed arms with fists clenched stationary in front of chest.

CLEARING

The back referee signals the clearing situation by fully extending his free arm (without whistle) over his head. The referee (or linesman) shall indicate the clearing is completed by extending his free arm over his head, up straight, and blowing his whistle.

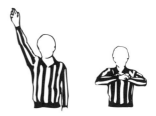

MISCONDUCT

Hands should be moved once from sides down to hips. Thus, point to player first, hands to hips second.

Figure 13.1
Referee signals

DELAYED OR SLOW WHISTLE

**PENALTY IN ONE-
REFEREE SYSTEM**
Use arm in which whistle is not held
(raising straight up). If play returns to
Neutral Zone without stoppage, arm
is drawn down the instant the
puck/ball crosses the line.

WASH-OUT

Both arms swung shoulder height,
not waist height.
1. When used by the referee it means "no
goal" and "no high-sticking the puck/ball."
2. When used by linesman it means "no clearing"
and/or "no high-sticking the puck/ball" only.
3. Used to indicate when a player deliberately
falls to the surface to draw a penalty.

DELAYED CALLING OF A PENALTY

PENALTY IN ONE-REFEREE SYSTEM
Referee raises arm to upright position. At stoppage of play, points
with free hand (free of whistle) with
palm open and fingers together.

DELAYED CALLING OF A PENALTY

Referee points with open palm,
fingers together, once with free
hand (without whistle).

TIMEOUT

Use both hands to form a "T" in front
of the chest.

TRIPPING

Keep both skates on the surface when signaling, using right hand on right leg.

INTENTIONAL OFFSIDE

After blowing whistle for offside, referee points toward offending team's special spot with non-whistle hand.

DELAY OF GAME

The nonwhistle hand, palm open, is placed across the chest, then fully extended directly in front of the body.

GOAL SCORED

The official points at the net with the nonwhistle hand, palm open, and blows the whistle.

HIGH-STICKING

Holding both fists clenched, one a short space immediately above the other, to the side of the head.

SLASHING

One chop with the nonwhistle hand across the straightened forearm of the other hand.

CROSS-CHECKING

A single forward and back motion with both fists clenched in front of the chest.

ROUGHING

Fist clenched, fully extending arm in front of the body. Checking will be considered a roughing penalty.

ELBOWING

Tap either elbow with the opposite hand.

BUTT-ENDING

A crossing motion of the forearms, one moving under the other.

CHARGING

Rotate clenched fists around one
another in front of chest.

PENALTY SHOT

Arms crossed (fists clenched)
above the head.

GRASPING THE FACE MASK

A single or double motion as if
grasping a face mask and pulling it
down.

SPEARING

A single jabbing motion with both
hands together, thrust forward in
front of the chest, then dropping
hands to the side.

KNEEING

A single slapping of the right palm
to the right knee, keeping both
skates on the surface.

■ DEFINITION OF TERMS

ABEC
Annular Bearing Engineering Council—Recognized developer of the scale of bearing quality.

ALLEN WRENCH
Tool used for securing the wheel axle to the skate frame.

ALTERCATION
Any physical action between two or more players resulting in penalties.

ALUMINUM SHAFT
A stick made of hollow foam-filled aluminum.

ANGLING
A skating pattern in which a skater moves toward the puck carrier on an angle and forces the carrier toward the boards.

ATTEMPT TO INJURE
A deliberate attempt to hurt another player. Match penalty.

BACK CHECK
A defensive action taken by a forward in the offensive zone while returning to the defensive zone.

BACKWARD PASS
A pass made with the back of the stick blade.

BACKWARD SHOT
A shot made with the back of the stick blade.

BEARINGS
The ring of ball bearings installed in each skate wheel.

BLADE
The bottom part of the stick used in handling or shooting the puck.

BLIND PASS
A pass made without looking.

BLOCKER MITT
The glove worn on the stick-holding hand of the goaltender.

BLOCKER SAVE
Type of blocked shot by the goalie using the blocker.

BREAKAWAY
A player having full control of the puck, with no opposition between the player and the opposing goal.

BREAKOUT
An offensive system for coming out of the defensive zone.

BUTT ENDING
The use of the shaft of the stick above the upper hand to jab another player.

CANTERING
Adjusting the skate frame laterally to maximize skating stride.

CAPTAIN
Player with C on jersey who represents the team with officials.

CATCHING GLOVE
A goaltender's glove used to catch the puck.

CHARGING
When a player takes two or more steps and makes contact with an opposing player.

CLEARING OF PUCK
Getting the puck out of the defensive zone.

COACH
The person responsible for directing and guiding the play of a team.

CORE
The center portion of a skate wheel.

CPR
Cardio-Pulmonary Resuscitation.

CREASES
Enclosed spaces designated for the protection of the goaltender and used by referees. The goalie crease is in front of the goal, and the referee crease is in front of the penalty timekeeper.

CROSS CHECKING
When a player with two hands on the stick checks an opponent with the shaft of the stick.

CROSSOVER
A turn in which the outside skate leaves the surface and crosses over the inner skate.

CSA
Canadian Safety Association.

CYCLING
A rotation of players in the defensive zone to maintain puck control and create scoring opportunities.

DEFLECTION
Redirecting a shot going toward the net.

DEKE
A fake by the puck carrier in the opposite direction from the carrier's intended route.

DELAYED WHISTLE
When a penalty occurs and the official does not stop the play until the defending team regains control of the puck.

DELAY OF GAME
A penalty for any delay in the game that is not necessary.

DROP PASS
Leaving the puck behind for a trailing teammate.

DUROMETER
A tool to measure the hardness of a wheel.

ELBOWING
Hitting the opponent with an elbow.

EMPTY NET
Any time in a game when the goaltender is not in the net.

FACE MASK
A wire or plastic shield worn by players to protect the face.

FACE-OFF
When a referee drops the puck to start a play.

FLIP SHOT
A shot used in close proximity to the net; to shoot the puck straight up to the top part of the net.

FORCE OUTSIDE
To force a defender to the boards away from the middle of the playing surface.

FULL STRENGTH
When both teams have all their skaters without penalties.

GIVE-AND-GO
A defensive tactic in which the puck is passed and the passer moves immediately for a return pass.

GOALTENDER
Person designated to stop the puck from entering the goal.

HAT TRICK
Three goals by one player in one game.

HEAD-MAN PASS
A pass by the puck carrier to a player ahead.

HECC
Hockey Equipment Certification Committee.

HIGH STICKING
When a player carries the stick above the waist.

HOLDING
When a player impedes the progress of an opposing player.

HOOKING
Using the stick blade to impede the progress of an opposing player.

HUB
The center of a skate wheel.

KICK SAVE
A save by a goaltender kicking a leg pad to prevent a goal.

KILLING A PENALTY
Preventing the other team from scoring on a power play.

KNOB
The top of the sticks shaft.

LANE
An open route between a passer and receiver.

LIE
The angle formed at the shaft and blade of the stick.

MAJOR PENALTY
A five-minute penalty.

MAN ADVANTAGE
When the opposing team is playing with fewer players because of a penalty.

MAN TO MAN COVERAGE
When a defensive player is responsible for a specific offensive player.

MINOR PENALTY
A two-minute penalty.

MISCONDUCT PENALTY
A ten-minute penalty.

NEUTRAL ZONE
Center part of the playing surface.

NIHA
National In-Line Hockey Association.

OFF WING
When a play is on the left side or vice versa.

PASS
The movement of the puck from one player to another.

PASSING ALLEY
A clear lane in which a pass can be made.

PENALTY
An infraction of the rules.

PENALTY BOX
Place players sit for penalties.

PICKING
To interfere with an opposing player, creating space for a teammate.

PINCHING
When a defensive player moves down to keep puck in the attacking zone.

POWER PLAY
The team with a man advantage is said to have a power play.

PROTECTIVE EQUIPMENT
Equipment worn to protect a player from injury.

PUCK
A piece of molded plastic used to play in-line roller hockey.

PULLING THE GOALIE
Removing the goalie in favor of an attacking forward.

QUIET ZONES
Space in the corners and behind net of the offensive zone, generally uncovered.

RAGGING
Retaining possession of the puck without the intention of scoring.

REBOUND
A puck that remains in play after coming off the goaltender.

REFEREE
The person supervising the game.

ROOFING THE PUCK
Shooting the puck up to the top part of the net from in close.

SAUCER PASS
A pass where the puck becomes airborne over a stick and lands flat on the other side.

SCREEN
A player positioned to block the goaltender's view.

SHADOWING
Closely guarding one specific player.

SHOOT-OUT
A system to break ties after regulation time has expired using shooter against goalie, one-on-one.

SHORT HANDED
Playing with fewer players than the other team, due to a penalty.

SKATE SAVE
A save made using the skate.

SLAP SHOT
Strongest shot used in in-line hockey. High wind-up, high follow-through.

SLASHING
Hitting another player with the stick.

SLOT
Area of playing surface in front of both nets where most scoring occurs.

SNAP SHOT
A shot produced by a low wind-up and low follow-through.

SPEARING
Poking a player with the point of the stick blade.

STAND UP GOALIE
A goalie who attempts to stand up as much as possible while stopping shots.

SWEEP CHECK
A flat sweeping motion of the stick to check an opponent.

TELEGRAPHING
When a player signals his or her intentions.

TIP IN
Redirecting a shot or pass into the goal.

TRANSITION
Quickly moving from offense to defense or vice versa.

WARM UP
A session to prepare team before actual play.

WRIST SHOT
A quick shot using the wrists.

Christian Jr./Sr. High School
2100 Greenfield Dr
El Cajon, CA 92019